1984

SO-AEG-750

THE IRAN-IRAQ WAR

Islam Embattled

STEPHEN R. GRUMMON

Foreword by Ambassador Robert G. Neumann

Published with The Center for
Strategic and International Studies,
Georgetown University, Washington, D.C.

PRAEGER SPECIAL STUDIES • PRAEGER SCIENTIFIC

Library of Congress Cataloging in Publication Data

Grummon, Stephen R., 1947–
    The Iran-Iraq war.

    (The Washington papers, ISSN 0278-937X ; 92)
    1. Iraqi-Iranian Conflict, 1980–   .
    2. Persian Gulf region—Strategic aspects.   I. Ti-
    tle. II. Series.
    DS318.8.G78   955′.054   82-5499
    ISBN 0-03-062011-2   AACR2

The opinions and views contained herein are those of the author and do not necessarily reflect the official views of the Department of State or of the Council on Foreign Relations.

The *Washington Papers* are written under the auspices of The Center for Strategic and International Studies (CSIS), Georgetown University, and published with CSIS by Praeger Publishers. The views expressed in these papers are those of the authors and not necessarily those of The Center.

Published in 1982 by Praeger Publishers
CBS Educational and Professional Publishing
a Division of CBS Inc.
521 Fifth Avenue, New York, New York 10175 U.S.A.

Contents

𝒪

Foreword

The Center for Strategic and International Studies is proud of its ability to anticipate important events and to study them before they hit the headlines. This paper by Stephen R. Grummon, which has been in preparation for many months, carries on that tradition.

To be sure, the war between Iran and Iraq was already underway when Mr. Grummon began his work. Public and media interest have fluctuated greatly, however. The public's attention was first alerted at the outbreak of the war because it was assumed that the flow of oil through the Persian Gulf would be endangered. It was also assumed that Iraq would win the war fairly easily, that the regime of the Ayatollah Ruhollah Khomeini would fall rapidly, and that Iran would be fractured into several parts. When this failed to occur, attention shifted elsewhere. More recently, there came the sudden discovery that, contrary to all expectation, Iran, not Iraq, was winning, and there was alarm over what that might mean to the stability of the region. Sudden discoveries of this kind, however, tend to be overdrawn and misleading.

It is to the author's credit that he not only accurately chronicles the history preceding the war and the war itself, but that he also puts it into perspective with regard to the belligerents, the region, and the world. He points out, briefly, that the general and territorial seeds of conflict were laid well in the past, especially during the rule of the Ottoman Empire. But then he shows that the Iran-Iraq war did not start primarily over these historical and geographic disputes, but that this war is largely ideological, which makes it particularly difficult to terminate. The war aims of both sides are not primarily military; the goal is the destruction of each other's political regime. In this, both sides adhere to their own clearly defined logic.

Grummon shows that the Khomeini regime in Iran adheres to a particular brand of theology that denies the legitimacy of most of the current governments in the Islamic world. Although this view first manifested itself in the opposition to the shah, the regime has made no bones about its conviction that it regards all the other regimes, especially those in the Persian Gulf, in the same light as that of the late shah. This condemnation is not at all a form of Sunni-Shi'a conflict, but is an Islamic command. Thus the Khomeini regime, both by its theological core and its revolutionary dynamics, is deeply destabilizing to the entire area.

That Iraq should feel the brunt of this threat particularly is also no accident, as Grummon points out. Quite apart from the long historical roots of the conflict, Iraq also aspired to regional leadership. Furthermore, Iraq's Ba'thist philosophy also questioned, less openly than did Khomeini, the legitimacy of existing regimes in the region. But in contrast to Khomeini's "mullocracy" Ba'thism is frankly secular and not specifically Islamic, which heightens the enmity between the two.

At the outset of the conflict, the moderate Arab states recognized that the destabilizing thrust from Iran was more immiment and dangerous than that from Iraq. Hence they placed themselves, with varying degrees of enthusiasm, on the side of Iraq. Yet Iraq's potential threat was sufficiently well recognized that they did not rush into the fray. Instead they let Baghdad carry the main burden of the struggle.

It came as a shock therefore, not only to the world but especially to the moderate Gulf states, that Iran, not Iraq, was gaining the upper hand. Yet, as of this moment, it is clearly premature to speak of an Iranian victory. Of course, in a political sense, one can say that the nature of the conflict is such that Iran wins if it does not lose and that Iraq loses if it does not win. But the Iranians have not occupied Baghdad, and their ability to do this is in doubt.

The author argues convincingly that the Iranian regime has demonstrated a remarkable ability to insulate the country's internal troubles from the conduct of the war. The Iraqi regime has managed to do this less well. Thus the war has created a new image and cohesion for the Iranian army and has also enhanced the standing and operation of the Revolutionary Guards. The Iranian army, under its young and largely unknown leadership, has become a potential force in a future internal power struggle; at the same time, the Revolutionary Guards have also enhanced their striking force and capability.

As Mr. Grummon delineates, the situation is quite different in Iraq. The Iraqi army's lacklustre performance is astonishingly bad and is clearly caused by its doctrine, training, and leadership for which President Saddam Husayn bears obvious responsibility. Mr. Grummon gives us the reasons and rationale without diminishing the impact that this failure may have on Saddam Husayn's leadership if and when credible opposition arises in the Iraqi army.

Whether or not the war drags on or leads to success for Iran, a clear victory for Iraq seems now excluded. One result, as the author underscores, has been the steady rise of

Saudi leadership in the region, which that country has applied with considerable skill and with hitherto uncharacteristic activism. But the Saudis know that as they become more prominent, they also become more vulnerable to those who hope to destabilize the region. In view of the vital importance of the area, it is inevitable that the two superpowers are increasingly drawn into the vortex of events. This study, then, is more than the analysis of a local conflict; it is a significant contribution to understanding a major source of destabilization of a vital region, a conflict that has global aspects and one that will continue to plague the world long after hostilities have ceased.

Robert G. Neumann
. Senior Associate, CSIS
. Former U.S. Ambassador to Morocco, Afghanistan, and Saudi Arabia
. May 1982

1

The Origin of the Conflict

The Historical Backdrop

Seen in a long-term historical perspective, the current Iran-Iraq war is just another phase in a struggle between the two countries that stretches back a millenium or more. Tension and rivalry have always existed between Iran and Iraq or their predecessors, in large part because the two countries lie on either side of a geographic and cultural divide. East of that divide is the vast Iranian plateau, which has been at the core of the Persian civilization. To the west lie the equally vast alluvial plains of the Tigris-Eurphrates river basin, which for the past 14 centuries have generally been dominated by a combination of Arab and Turkish rulers. Although the two antagonists are in theory united by an ecumenical Islamic civilization, nevertheless, political and cultural tensions have continued to be the hallmark of their relations. Thus, the modern political border that separates them merely provides de jure recognition of this ancient de facto reality.

Underlying the political tension and rivalry is a clash of what might be termed cultural nationalisms. Very broadly speaking, the Persian heartland is dominated by descend-

1

ants of Indo-European tribes who speak Farsi (Persian), an Indo-European language. Iraq on the other hand is composed primarily (although by no means exclusively) of Semitic peoples who speak Arabic, a Semitic language.

Islam itself has also had a tendency to divide the two countries rather than acting as a unifying force. For approximately four and a half centuries, Iran has been the bastion of the Shi'ite branch of Islam, while Iraq's political elites have oriented that country toward Sunni Islam. Moreover, both Arabs and Persians remember that it was the Arabs who conquered Iran and gave Islam to the Persians, but that it was Persian civilization that took raw, desert Islam and refined and tempered it much as raw Christianity was tempered by Greek culture and that provided many of the underpinnings for the classical Islamic civilization that flowered in subsequent centuries.

The preceding generalizations are laced with anomalies, like so many generalizations made about the Middle Eastern social and cultural map. The descendants of Arabs, for example, live in Iran, particularly in the province of Khuzistan and along the Persian Gulf coast line as far south as Bandar Lengeh and Bandar Abbas. By the same token, large communities of Persians or descendants of Persians can be found in Iraq. (In 1980, Iraqi President Saddam Husayn expelled some 40 thousand of these Persians from Iraq.) Nor are religious lines clear cut and distinct. Shi'ites actually make up a majority of Iraq's population, although Iraq's political and economic elites are not drawn from their ranks. In addition, Shi'ite Islam's holiest shrines and sanctuaries are found in the Iraqi cities of Karbala and Najaf, not in Iran. For its part, Iran cannot be considered a totally Shi'ite country. Most of the minorities who inhabit the peripheries of the country (e.g., the Kurds, Arabs, Turkomans, and Baluchis) are Sunni in orientation. (Again there are exceptions to the preceding statement; for example, there are both Shi'ite and Sunni Kurds and Shi'ite and Sunni Arabs.)

These social and cultural differences have provided the backdrop against which repeated political clashes have occurred. The modern history of these conflicts began with the Ottoman-Safivid rivalries in the sixteenth century. These rivalries continued into the eighteenth century and were most vividly manifested by Nadir Shah's seige of Mosul and Baghdad in 1734 and Karim Khan Zand's capture of Basra in 1774. Although tension and border skirmishes continued into the nineteenth century, the situation became more stable under the prodding of Great Britain, and joint survey teams were commissioned to demarcate the border.

Contemporary rivalries have continued to involve localized territorial and border issues. In the twentieth century, the most dramatic problem has been centered around the issue of sovereignty over the Shatt al Arab river. The Shatt is approximately 130 miles in length and is formed by the joining of the Tigris and Euphrates rivers. For the last 55 miles of its journey to the Persian Gulf, the Shatt forms the border between Iraq and Iran. Approximately 45 miles north of the mouth of the Shatt it is joined by Iran's most important river system, the Karun. (See maps 1 and 2.)

The Shatt and the region around it have strategic and economic importance for both countries, but particularly for Iraq. The Shatt is Iraq's principal maritime window on the world, its "warm water port," to draw an analogy from Russian history. Basra, virtually the only Iraqi commercial port of any importance, lies about 47 miles up the Shatt. Major crude oil export pipelines lie parallel to the river, often at a close distance, and a major crude tank farm is situated at al-Faw, on the Gulf near the mouth of the river.

The political and physical geography of the northern reaches of the Persian Gulf strongly suggests that Basra will remain Iraq's preeminent port and that the Shatt will therefore remain Iraq's major economic artery for an indefinite period of time. For example, the country has less than a 50-mile coastline on the Gulf, most of which is low, swampy,

Map 1

Map 2

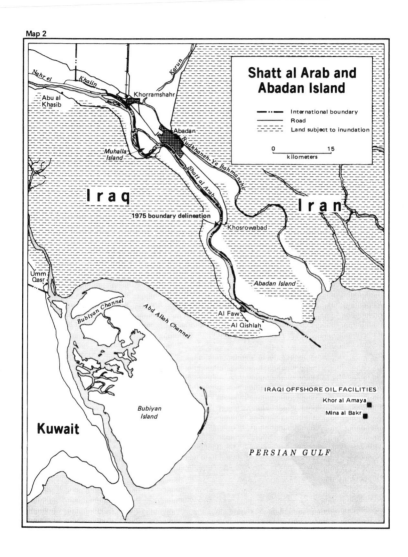

Shatt al Arab and Abadan Island

— · · · —	International boundary
———	Road
- - - - -	Land subject to inundation

0   15
kilometers

Nahr el   Khalin   Karun

Abu al
Khasib

Khorramshahr

Abadan

Muhalla
Island

Rudkhaneh-Ye Bahmanshir

Shatt al Arab

I r a q

1975 boundary delineation

I r a n

Khosrowabad

Umm
Qasr

Bubiyan Channel

Abd Allah Channel

Abadan Island

Al Faw
Al Qishlah

Bubiyan
Island

Kuwait

IRAQI OFFSHORE OIL FACILITIES

Khor al Amaya

Mina al Bakr

PERSIAN GULF

and generally ill suited for port development. (The cost of infrastructual development would be staggering.) Although there is a port at Umm Qasr (on the western extremity of the Iraqi Gulf coast), it, too, lies in swampy terrain and is approached from the Gulf through a narrow channel commanded by the Kuwaiti islands of Warbah and Bubiyan.

Thus, Claudia Wright, the British journalist, is correct when she argues that "from the Iraqi point of view, hostile hands are always potentially around the country's throat."[1] Iraq believes that its most important economic and, hence, strategic assets are unprotected because Iraq lacks strategic, territorial depth.

Iran, too, has important economic interests on the Shatt. For decades its most important port has been Khorramshahr, which lies at the confluence of the Shatt and Karun rivers and which also serves the southern railhead for the Trans-Iranian railway system. Despite Iran's long coastline, geography and transportation economics will continue to assure a prominent place for Khorramshahr in Iran's commercial life. Physically, it is the port closest to the major inland population centers. Commercially, transporting goods up the Gulf by ship and then loading them at the Khorramshahr railhead for the journey inland is still cheaper than off-loading at a more southerly port.

Although the Shatt has an obvious economic importance for Iran, the river does not present the country with the same strategic vulnerabilities that it does Iraq. Iran's major petroleum export facilities are not in the immediate area, and Iran has other usable Persian Gulf ports. Prior to the war, the Abadan refinery, which lies on the Shatt, was Iran's most important refinery, supplying the country with some 60 percent of its required domestic refined product. It is doubtful, however, if Abadan will ever again play such a prominent role in the country's energy requirements. Rather than rebuild the badly damaged refinery on the same site, the Iranians are likely to move further inland should they decide to construct a new facility.

Sovereignty over the Shatt al Arab region was a point of contention between the Ottoman and Persian governments. Both laid claim to vast tracts of territory on either side of the river, as tribes living in the region professed loyalty first to one government and then to the other. By the nineteenth century, however, the general outline of the border had been defined: Land east of the Shatt belonged to Iran, while territory to the west belonged to the Ottomans and to Iraq as the successor state. A precise border was not demarcated during the nineteenth century however.

The growth of commerce in the area in the late nineteenth and early twentieth centuries and the discovery of oil in Khuzistan in 1908 dramatically increased the pressure for a more precise delineation of the boundary. In 1913, a series of negotiations produced the Constantinople Accords. These negotiations drew the boundary at the low water mark of the eastern (Iranian) shore line. Iran remained dissatisfied with the outcome of the 1913 accords and a new treaty was negotiated in 1937 that modified the boundary line around Abadan. In that area, the border was drawn according to the thalweg principle.[2] The rest of the border, however, remained along the low water mark of the eastern shore in accordance with the provision of the 1913 accord. In 1975, yet another treaty was negotiated that adopted the thalweg principle as the basis for demarcating the entire Shatt al Arab border. It is that treaty that Saddam Husayn declared null and void just prior to Iraq's invasion of Iran on September 22, 1980.

Territorial and border disputes are not the only questions dividing Iraq and Iran: Ideological rivalry has been an equally divisive and explosive issue in the relations between the two countries, particularly in the post-World War II era. In its first phase, this rivalry pitted radical Arab socialism, including Iraqi Ba'thism against the shah. Iraqi Ba'thism would rejuvinate the Arab nation, in part by sweeping away the archaic political system (that is, the monarchies) that prevailed on both sides of the Gulf. In opposition, the shah saw himself as a defender and protector of the regional status quo. He was singularly determined to prevent the export of Iraqi political influence and power.

Although the Iranian revolution may have shifted the focus of some of the issues in the ideological debate, it has not lessened the intensity of the rivalry.[3] The tables have now turned, however, with the Ayatollah Ruhollah Khomeini now denouncing the status quo. Khomeini has repeatedly declared that Ba'thism is a "Satanic" philosophy and has sworn to destroy it, along with Saddam Husayn. He has also declared the various Gulf governments illegitimate. In reality, this ideological rivalry masks a larger issue: Both countries want to be the Gulf's paramount power. Ideology is an important component in a drive for domination.

The Origins of the Current Conflict

This study makes no attempt to apportion blame for the war, although it does seem that both sides should stand condemned for initiating a series of such inflammatory actions as border provocations and the support of internal dissidence, which eventually lead to the outbreak of the war. Only Iraq, however, had the ability to escalate the conflict to a full-scale war. Iran was certainly capable of raising the level of tensions during the border-skirmishing phase of the confrontation. Nevertheless, Iran was not prepared to go to war with Iraq, given the fundamentalist leadership's paranoid attitude toward the military and its preoccupation with the hostage crisis. It would have to be Iraq that would escalate the limited border hostilities to full-scale war.[4]

Besides the immediate cycle of border violence that occurred in the months preceding the commencement of full scale hostilities, there were several political factors that probably predisposed Baghdad to consider total war. In fact, the underlying origins of the war probably were rooted in four events and the ramifications that flowed from them. The Iranian Revolution was probably the single most important event paving the way for the war. In rapid order Iran was transformed from "an island of stability" into a caldron of chaos and turmoil following the shah's collapse, the decimation of much of the high level officer corps in the military and police, and the emergence of a vicious power struggle among the victorious revolutionaries. The revolution had two important spin-offs for Iraq. First, it contained an inherent danger for the Ba'thi regime. A revolutionary ideology quickly emerged that, in its foreign policy dimension, is clearly revisionist. Specifically, Iran has vigorously condemned and encouraged the overthrow of secular political leaders such as Saddam Husayn. These ideological currents could not be lightly ignored by the Ba'this, because a majority of Iraq's population are Shi'ite—although admittedly Arab Shi'ites. Nevertheless, one Shi'ite revolution could encourage another. The seizure of the American Embassy and the subsequent triumph of the radicals over the moderates in Iran probably convinced Baghdad that such foreign policy predispositions would not be brought under control.[5]

Second, the growing chaos that occurred in Iran during 1979 and 1980 probably created the impression in Baghdad that Iran was weak and vulnerable. Surveying the Iranian scene in the months preceding the war, Baghdad believed Iran was incapable of defending its interests and was isolated diplomatically, particularly in the Gulf region and also from its major arms patron, the United States. The balance of power appeared to have shifted decisively (although not necessarily permanently) in Iraq's favor.

Along with the fear of the revolution, another factor encouraged Iraq to act: the opportunity to revise the results of the 1975 treaty, which had been negotiated under the auspices of the Algerians. In theory, the treaty was to have settled all outstanding differences between Tehran and Baghdad, particularly border problems. In particular, the treaty called for two broad categories of border adjustments. In the central border area, Iran was supposed to return to Iraq several disputed parcels of territory, which Tehran had not done, while the thalweg principle was to be applied to the Shatt border.

Saddam Husayn, who was Iraq's chief treaty negotiator, considered the treaty a personal humiliation, and he had negotiated it only under pressure. The negotiations were conducted under duress because at the time the shah was actively aiding and abetting a Kurdish rebellion in northern Iraq. As long as this Iranian support, with its strong component of military aid, continued, there was little likelihood that Baghdad would be able to contain, much less supress, the uprising. Because some of Iraq's major oil fields lay on the immediate periphery of the Kurdish area, however, Baghdad had an obvious interest in bringing the rebellion under control. The thalweg concession on the Shatt was the *quid pro quo* Baghdad had to pay for a termination of Iranian aid to the Kurds.

The treaty relaxed tensions in the first two or three years following its signing. Nevertheless the conditions under which the treaty was negotiated suggested that an inherently unstable relationship had only been stabilized temporarily rather than permanently altered. Saddam Husayn almost certainly hoped to revise the treaty. Moreover, continued adherence to the treaty depended on Iran's ability to maintain a preponderance of political and military power.

Third, the Camp David accords provided a catalyst that helped lay the ground work leading to the outbreak of hostilities. When Egypt signed the accords, it forfeited its leader-

ship role in the Arab world. Saddam Husayn, who eagerly
sought to fill the leadership vacuum left by the Egyptian de-
fection, seized the initiative by sponsoring the Baghdad
Summits. Although the Summits were notable achieve-
ments, by the fall of 1980 Husayn had yet to orchestrate
successfully an event or series of events that would validate
beyond all doubt his bid to be the Arab world's chief spokesman. In other words, Saddam Husayn had not yet found an
event similar to the 1955 seizure of the Suez Canal that
would catapult him to the forefront of Arab leadership.

Finally, the regional political and diplomatic positions
of the superpowers may have affected the Iraqi decision to
go to war. The United States was preoccupied with the hostage crisis and would not support the Khomeini regime, and
the Soviet Union was bogged down in Afghanistan. Moreover, the U.S. reaction to the Soviet invasion of Afghanistan
virtually guaranteed that the two superpowers would not
work together to impose a ceasefire on the two conflicting
parties in favor of the status quo. Thus, Iraq would be able
to dictate peace terms following the military victory. There
was a risk, of course, that the Soviets would wholeheartedly
support Iran in the conflict. Baghdad may have calculated,
however, that Khomeini would not be responsive to any Soviet overtures.

Combined, these factors created the atmosphere in
which the decision was made to invade Iran. They also provided the basis of Iraq's original war aims. Iraq, still smart-
ing from a humiliating treaty, saw an opportunity to restore
the border to its "rightful" location. By seizing a substantial chunk of Khuzistan, which could be used as a bargaining
chip in any future Shatt negotiations, a fatal blow would be
delivered to the Khomeini regime. The collapse of the regime, which would follow as a matter of course, would eliminate a movement abhorred by all the region. Thus, Iraq
would emerge as the paramount protector of the Arabian

Peninsula states, the Gulf's preeminent military force, and the defender of the Arab homeland. The three islands occupied by Iran in 1971 would be returned to the United Arab Emirates (UAE) in the course of negotiations, and the Arabs of Khuzistan might be liberated or given much greater autonomy within Iran. On a wider scale, Saddam Husayn, having found his "Suez Canal," could emerge as the leader of the Arab cause against Israel.

The Escalation of Hostilities

Relations between the two countries had quickly deteriorated following the collapse of the shah's regime. Two issues served as a lightning rod for this collapse and were at the center of the increasing hostilities. First, both sides charged that the other was meddling in its internal affairs with the expressed intent of hoping to overthrow the other. Iranian propaganda broadcasts, increased agitation and ferment in the Shi'ite sections of Iraqi villages, towns, and cities, and bombings and assassination attempts were cited as evidence to support the Iraqi claims. Iran, on the other hand, pointed to agitation by Iranian Arabs in Khuzistan and repeated pipeline explosions as evidence that Iraq was interfering in its internal affairs. The Iranians also saw an Iraqi hand behind developments in Kurdistan. Fighting between the Kurds and the Revolutionary Guard began within two months of the victory of the revolutionaries and has continued on a more or less permanent basis ever since. Tehran was convinced that Baghdad was supplying the Kurds with food and with military, medical, and financial aid.

The second point of contention was the border. In the year or so following the shah's collapse, border clashes had periodically occurred. In the weeks prior to the outbreak of the war, however, the tempo, intensity, and scope of the clashes quickened. For example, between August 28 and September 3, 1980, Baghdad claimed to have repulsed 14 Iranian attacks. The Iraqi broadcasts noted that "heavy and medium artillery and mortars" had been used in the exchanges and that the fighting in some cases had lasted up to 35 minutes.[6] Concurrently, the Iranians were countering the Iraqi charges with their own claims: In August 1980, Iraq had positioned up to 300 tanks in the area opposite Qasr-e Shirin. Moreover, by the end of August, the Iranian governor of Kermanshah province claimed that Iraqi shelling of towns such as Naft-e Shah and Qasr-e Shirin was so severe that civilians were being forced to evacuate them. In turn, the Iraqis charged that the Iranians had shelled the towns of Mandali and Khanaqin on September 4.

On September 10, Baghdad expanded the scale and scope of the fighting with the forceful seizure around Zayn al-Qaws and Sayf Sa'ad of strips of territory that had been occupied by Iran for several decades but under the terms of the 1975 treaty were to have been returned to Iraq. The Iraqis easily seized these areas, routing the Iranians in less than a full day of fighting.

On the same day of this operation, Iraqi Foreign Minister Sa'dun Hammadi explained to the press that the territory belonged to Iraq under the terms of the treaty and that when the Iranian revolution occurred, Baghdad had been willing to give the new government time to establish itself before pressing the issue again. Iran, however, had shown no inclination to fulfill its obligations, but instead had displayed hostile intentions.

Hammadi also revealed that Baghdad had delivered two notes to the Iranian chargé, apparently on September 7 and 8. In the first, Baghdad explained the Iranian violation of the terms of the treaty and demanded an evacuation of the territory. Then on the eighth, Baghdad warned Tehran that it intended to seize the territory.[7] Two days later Baghdad made good on its threat.

As far as is known, the Iranians did not respond to the Iraqi notes until September 13, fully three days after the occupation of Zayn al-Qaws and Sayf Sa'ad. In a radio broadcast, the Iranian Ministry of Foreign Affairs skirted the issue of Iranian responsibility for evacuating the territories under the 1975 agreement. Instead, it focused on Iraqi enmity toward the revolution and Iraq's failure to confront the Zionist enemy. In a curious reference to the 1975 treaty, the broadcast did refer to "the lands which according to the 1975 agreement belonged to Iraq but over which it has not been able to establish its sovereignty," (FBIS comment: "as heard").[8] Tehran, however, refused to acknowledge that it should evacuate the territories.

Events now moved quickly. The fighting expanded to the Shatt al Arab region. According to Iraqi broadcasts, artillery exchanges across the Shatt occurred on September 11 and then again on the 15th, while Iranian communiqués indicated exchanges also took place on the 13th and 14th.

Then on September 17, Saddam Husayn abrogated the 1975 treaty.[9] According to Iraqi thinking, with the treaty abrogated, "the legal relationship concerning [the] Shatt al-Arab should return to what it was before 6 March, 1975. This Shatt shall again be, as it has been throughout history, Iraqi and Arab in name and reality, with all right of full soverignty over it."[10]

Iran would never acquiesce in the Iraqi move. Moreover, it was capable of making a mockery of the declaration, because it could easily prevent Iraq from using the river—a fact that Husayn knew when he made the speech. Thus, the political and military status quo had to be altered. Iran had to be forced to acknowledge the Iraqi claims. The invasion of Khuzistan would be the instrument of persuasion.

2

The Course of the War: Goals, Strategy, and Campaigns

Wars have to be justified; their goals and purposes explained to the home population, the enemy, and to the outside world. Both Iraq and Iran were quick to explain and defend their war aims once the fighting escalated to full-scale hostilities. On September 28, 1980, Saddam Husayn outlined Iraq's initial war aims by demanding that Iran

• recognize Iraq's legitimate and soverign rights over its land and waters (that is, the Shatt al Arab);

• refrain from interfering in Iraq's (and other regional states') internal affairs;

• adhere to the principle of good neighborly relations; and

• return to the United Arab Emirates the Iranian-occupied islands in the Persian Gulf.[11]

As the Iraqi military position in Khuzistan gradually worsened during the spring of 1982, Baghdad shifted the emphasis in the war's purpose. It was now claimed that the central goal of the war was to check Iranian expansionism and that that goal was being accomplished. Iraqi retreates were justified not because of military pressure or defeat but on the basis that Iraq had achieved its objective of inflicting the highest possible losses on Iran "to stop it from continuing with its blatant aggressive and expansionist plans."

The Iranians had a sliding scale of demands. At a minimum, Iraq would have to end its aggression. In a September 26 interview, President Abulhassan Bani-Sadr noted that "we are being attacked, and so to end this aggression, it is Iraq which will have to take steps; it is Iraq which will have to end its aggression i.e. through an unconditional withdrawal."[12] Iraq would also have to acknowledge its war guilt and pay reparations. But Iranian objectives go deeper. According to the Ayatollah Khomeini, "the war against Iran is a war against Islam, it is a war against the Koran, it is a war against the prophet of God."[13] The purpose of the war, therefore, was to facilitate the overthrow of the Ba'thi regime. Early in the war, Prime Minister Muhammad Ali Rajai stated, "We thank God that the enemies of the Islamic Revolution have themselves dug their graves by the hands of the people because of their attacks . . .God wants us to share, together with the nation of Iraq, in the honor of toppling Saddam and his executioner regime."[14] There has been virtually no modification in the demands of either side since the early days of the war.

The Strategy and Tactics of the War

Saddam Husayn was probably planning for war throughout the spring and summer of 1980.[15] On the military side, Wright claims that,

> Iraq's initial war plan was as simple as the classic seige tactics of ancient Mesopotamia. It was to destroy

Iran's oil sources, refineries and transportation routes, and by cutting these off from the rest of the country to put the political regime in Tehran in a vise from which neither it nor the Iranian people could break free.[16]

If Wright's description accurately describes the Iraqi grand strategy, then in fact Baghdad failed to adhere to the plan. Although Iraqi forces initially moved very rapidly into central and southern Iran, nevertheless, by the third or fourth day of fighting, the Iraqi advances in Khuzistan had stopped from 15 to 20 kilometers short of Khuzistan's more important urban centers. Cities such as Ahvaz or Dezful were never placed under serious seige. (Long-range artillery bombardments of these cities do not constitute a seige sufficient to force their surrender.) Moreover, although most of Khorramshahr has been occupied and Abadan threatened, the capture of these cities would have only marginally contributed to an overall Iraqi strategic victory.[17]

Baghdad also failed to seize or cut strategic installations such as the oil pipelines and the railroad that run north through Dezful. More important, there is no indication that Husayn ever contemplated striking at the heart of Iran's petroleum center—the oil fields themselves and the Marun pipeline, which alone has the capacity to feed crude stocks to all of Iran's refineries in the hinterlands.

Nor has Husayn been able to pressure the Iranians with air or naval power while maintaining his "seige." Theoretically, Iraqi airpower should have contributed to the ground effort by bombing refineries, pumping stations, and transport facilities. In fact, though, in the early phases of the war, much of the Iraqi air force was flown to safe haven in other Arab countries. Moreover, when the air force has been used, it has been only marginally effective. On the water, the Iranian navy has been totally dominant.

At best, Iran has been put under a partial seige—an action that has not proved sufficient to compel the Iranians to respond to Iraqi demands. Although it is impossible to describe with accuracy Baghdad's precise military thinking, actual Iraqi military behavior seems to suggest that Baghdad assumed that merely driving into Khuzistan would be sufficient to produce a quick, relatively cheap victory. The Iraqi attack was primarily an armored thrust, and, although armor can move quickly and take great swaths of territory, it cannot take cities. Husayn may have calculated that the shock of the attack would be enough to topple Khomeini and force the Iranians to negotiate on his terms. Thus Iraqi actions do not appear to have been formulated more on the basis of specific Iraqi strategic objectives such as seizure of the oil fields or the Marun pipeline, which would force the "correct" Iranian response. Such a strategy is akin to developing a master plan in chess that culminates in a check mating sequence but which depends upon one's opponent making the "right" move so that the plan can be put into action. Such a move is rarely made among good chess players.

Although it was clear by mid-November 1980 that Iran would not collapse under the impact of the Iraqi attack, Iraq failed to develop a coherent strategy and corresponding set of tactics to take into account a determined Iranian adversary, yet produce the strategic victory—that is, a victory that would force the Iranians to negotiate on Iraqi terms. Several factors account for this situation: Saddam Husayn's unwillingness to pay the high price in casualties and equipment, a necessary price if Iran were to be defeated militarily, and the lack of obvious strategic targets in Khuzistan that would produce a military victory, other than seizure of the oil fields. In the latter case, Iraq probably does not have the logistical capability to seize and hold them.

From time to time, Iraq has employed what might be termed bogus tactics in an apparent effort to force the Iranians to the negotiating table. Thus, in the spring of 1981,

Husayn threatened to assist in the dismemberment of Iran by supporting ethnic minorities such as the Kurds, the Arabs of Khuzistan, and even the Baluch. Husayn, however, was in no position to play such a card seriously because of the Kurds in his own backyard. (Kurdish independence movements can be contagious.) Moreover, in the case of the Iranian Arabs, by the time Husayn raised the dismemberment issue, it was patently clear that the Arabs supported Iran, rather than Iraq. The allegiance of the majority of Iranian Arabs to Tehran rather than Baghdad has been one of the surprises of the war.[18]

Long-range missile attacks on urban centers such as Ahvaz or Dezful have produced equally meager results. If anything, they have reinforced Iranian determination to resist rather than producing the hoped for sag in morale. Thus, after well over a year of hostilities, Iraq was saddled with a long, static military front that is vulnerable to Iranian counterattack. Moreover, it is incapable of putting the Tehran regime in a vice-like grip and then delivering the much hoped for political victory.

The Iranians responded to the Iraqi attack in a straightforward manner. The major emphasis was on defense, thus, Tehran concentrated on trying to stabilize the front line while building up and reinforcing defensive positions. During the winter and spring of 1981, the heavy rains in Khuzistan and the subsequent flooding were effectively employed in this defensive effort. Concurrently, the Iranian Revolutionary Guards, or *Pasdaran*, conducted nighttime hit and run raids behind the Iraqi lines in an effort to disrupt logistical support efforts.[19] Such raids, however, have not had a significant negative impact on the operations of the Iraqi logistical machine.

A second prong of the Iranian response, however, was offensive in nature: Tehran deliberately decided to take the war to the oil fields, despite early indications out of Baghdad that it would be willing to exempt the oil sector from the war.[20] The Iranian decision, probably made within the first 24 hours of the war, appears to have been motivated by the desire to demonstrate to both populations in as highly visible a manner as possible that the Iranian military machine was still functioning, while striking at a point where Husayn was most vulnerable. Thus, Iranian air and naval power was able to shut down temporarily all Iraqi exports. Although Iraq is now able to export through its northern pipelines, its exports through the Gulf, which accounted for about two-thirds of Iraqi exports prior to the war, remain suspended due to Iranian naval superiority and the damage that Iraq's two offshore loading facilities sustained in November 1980. A third prong of the Iranian response appeared much later in the war: Tehran began to probe and jab at the static Iraqi line in an effort to seize the initiative, albeit thus far a limited initiative.

Two distinct groups have defended Iran: the professional military and the paramilitary Revolutionary Guards. Until the war began, the military had been reeling under the impact of clerical-directed purges, forced retirements, executions, and the loss of those fleeing the country. The size of the military had dramatically decreased from approximately 450 thousand to perhaps under 200 thousand. Moreover, training and weapons maintenance had been neglected.

The Revolutionary Guards is composed of young men who were born in the 1950s and 1960s. They are generally from urban areas and are from lower middle and working class backgrounds. Few members of the Guards have attended a university, although many of them appear to have completed high school. The Revolutionary Guards have been closely identified with the fundamentalist clerics, acting as their agents both at the national and local level. More specifically, the Guards have tended to be the creature of the Islamic Republican Party (IRP) and were employed effectively by the party in its struggle with Bani-Sadr and other anti-IRP politicians and opposition groups such as the Mujahedin-e Khalq.

Very broadly speaking, the military and the Guards have carried out separate wartime duties. The military has conducted the air strikes, naval operations, and armored maneuvers. It has also generally been in charge of the heavy artillery. The Guards have been responsible for hit and run raids and have been the main force that has assaulted various Iraqi positions (often successfully). Consequently, Revolutionary Guards losses have been heavy. Relations between the two groups have not always been harmonious, although recent Iranian campaigns suggest that coordination between them may be improving.

Following the freezing of the battle lines in the first week or so of hostilities, the war settled into a fairly routine pattern consisting of long-range artillery duels, air strikes on oil and other targets, which have gradually dissipated, although not ceased altogether, and nighttime raids. Although Saddam Husayn boasted about a spring offensive in 1981, that Iraqi attack failed to materialize, largely for reasons previously outlined—a probably high casualty rate with no assurance of winning the strategic victory. The tactical initiative has now passed to Iran—where it remains.

Military Operations

There have been three discernible phases in the war: the Iraqi offensive, which started on September 22, 1980 and ended approximately in mid-November, the stalemate, which lasted from mid-November to early May 1981, and the Iranian counteroffensive, which began in May 1981 and is continuing.[21]

The war opened with a three-front Iraqi invasion of

Iran: In the south, Iraq moved into Khuzistan; in the central sector, Iraqi forces occupied a belt of territory from Qasr-e Shirin and Sar-e Pol-e Zohab in the north to Mehran in the south. In the far north, another front was opened along the border area opposite Sulaymaniyah. (See map 3.) The Khuzistan front has been the scene of the majority of the more important offensives and counteroffensives.

Map 3

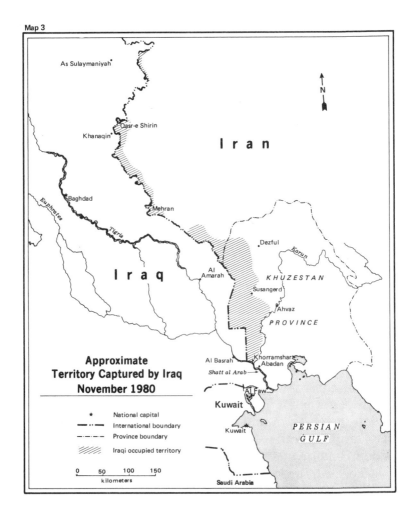

The invasion of Khuzistan was launched from two Iraqi cities: al-Amarah and Basra. From al-Amarah, Iraqi forces crossed the border and moved in two directions: toward Dezful and down the Bostan-Susangerd road toward Ahvaz, the provincial capital of Khuzistan. The Iraqis voluntarily stopped their advance in front of both cities and in both cases made no attempt to cross the main channel of the Karun river. From Basra, the Iraqi army crossed the border at several points, again heading for two basic objectives: Ahvaz and the Khorramshahr/Abadan area.

Although the Iranians from time to time had claimed that Iraq was preparing to attack, they truly seemed to have been caught off guard when the actual invasion came.[22] Border outposts such as those at Bostan were too indefensible, ill-equipped, and undermanned to resist a full-scale invasion. These stations were only prepared to carry out border skirmishes, which had characterized the earlier phase of tensions. Thus, there was only token Iranian resistence, with most Iranian forces quickly falling back to cities such as Ahvaz and Dezful.

During this phase of the war, the Iraqis primarily fixed their attention on the Khorramshahr/Abadan region and made a concerted effort to seize those two cities. The Khorramshah/Abadan area is surprisingly defensible, despite appearances to the contrary. Three rivers dominate the region: the Shatt al Arab, the Karun, and the Bahmanshir. Khorramshahr sits at the confluence of the Karun and Shatt al Arab and can be readily approached only from a northerly direction. On the other hand, Abadan, which is approximately eight miles south of Khorramshahr, is actually located on Abadan island, which is formed by the three rivers. Its defensibility is further enhanced by the fact that the area south of the Karun and east of the Bahmanshir is low, swampy, and subject to flooding.

In preparing to take the two cities, the Iraqis moved heavy artillery up to the western edge of the Shatt al Arab and subjected the cities to heavy shelling. The Iraqi army itself approached the area from the northwest. Within a matter of days it quickly gained control of the northern approaches to Khorramshahr because the Iranian military made little effort to defend the cities by engaging the Iraqis in the desert spaces to the north.

The Iranians, however, were not prepared to give up Khorramshahr itself without a desperate fight, and it took Iraq approximately a month to subdue the city. The fighting, which was extremely bloody, was conducted on a street by street, house by house basis, starting in the northwestern quadrant of the city and gradually moving toward the old bazaar section in the southeastern portion of the town. A bridge connects the bazaar area to Abadan island and the town of Abadan; it was through this link that the Iranian forces in Khorramshahr were reinforced and resupplied.

Until late October, Iraqi forces remained north of the Karun river. In preparation for the Abadan campaign, however, the Iraqis crossed the Karun several miles east of Khorramshahr toward the end of October 1980. They quickly cut the road that linked Abadan with Bandar Khomeini (formerly Bandar Shahpur) and prepared to shell and starve Abadan into submission. They did not attempt a frontal assault on the oil town by crossing onto the island from Khorramshahr or from the east across the Bahmanshir.

Abadan, however, did not fall. It was able to hold out primarily because the Iranians were in fact able to resupply the city by moving supplies up the Bahmanshir. Thus Iranian naval superiority in the Gulf played a vital role in the defense of Abadan, because Iraq had no hope of cutting off this resupply channel. Under these circumstances, if Iraq were to capture Abadan, an assault on the city was absolutely necessary; bombardment alone could not force the Iranians to capitulate. Saddam Husayn, however, was apparently unwilling to risk an assault.

Toward the end of the first phase of the war, the shape of the battle front had the rough appearance of a reversed number three, with the major concentration of Iraqi forces before Dezful, Ahvaz, and in and around the Khorramshahr/ Abadan complex. Between Dezful and Ahvaz another concentration of forces lay along the Susangerd-Hamidiyeh axis. Each side was able to move freely behind its lines.

In the central sector, Iraq moved quickly in the opening days of the war to seize the Iranian towns of Qasr-e Shirin, the mountain heights around Sar-e Pol-e Zohab, and other strategic points further south in the Mehran region. Further north a narrow border strip was apparently seized opposite Sulaymaniyah. Repeated Iranian attempts to dislodge the Iraqis from these areas have failed to produce any substantive results.

From the Iraqi perspective, it has been vitally important to hold these strategic points in this sector. The heights around Qasr-e Shirin dominate the Iraqi lowlands, and the town itself sits astride the road to Baghdad, which is approximately 80 miles to the southeast. If the Iranians broke through to the Iraqi lowlands in this area, the road to Baghdad would be open. Although it is unlikely that the Iranians would attempt to carry the campaign to the Iraqi capital, the Iraqis could not afford to leave the way open. The Iraqi southern flank in Khuzistan could also be threatened because Iraqi forces in the south would almost surely have to redeploy north. Such a move would weaken the position of the remaining troops in Khuzistan.

By mid-November 1980, the war had settled into a stalemate, which was characterized by long-range artillery duels, continuing air strikes on oil and other targets (which gradually dissipated), and nighttime sabotage raids conducted mainly by the Iranian Revolutionary Guards.

Several factors combined to produce this stalemate: First, Iraqi military strategy and tactics failed to capitalize on Baghdad's advantage of surprise. Second, Iran did not collapse, and Baghdad was unsure about an alternative course of action. Third, Iran was still reeling under the impact of the initial Iraqi assault. Before it could hope to launch any initiative of its own, Iran needed time to reorganize and deploy forces and supplies. The fourth factor was the weather. Although it is not often recognized, the Khuzistan region is subject to winter rains and flooding. The flooding is the result of both the runoff from the rains and, during the spring, from the melting snow in the Zagros mountains. As a result, much of Khuzistan turns into a sea of mud, making it difficult—if not virtually impossible—for wheeled or tracked vehicles to move except on paved roads. As it turned out, the flooding in 1980–1981 was particularly severe.

During the stalemate there was one major offensive—the ill-conceived Iranian thrust in the Susangerd region. In that sector, the Iranians were surrounded on three sides by Iraqi forces. There was also a concentration of Iranian forces lying to the southeast of the southern flank of the Iraqi forces. The Iranians apparently hoped to split the Iraqi line and envelop the eastern half of this line in a pincer movement. Accordingly, Iranian forces drove deeply into the Iraqi line, penetrating almost as far as Hoveyzeh. Concurrently, Iranian forces lying southeast of the Iraqi concentrations attacked. Although the Iranian drive seemed initially successful, the following day the Iraqis counterattacked, demolishing the Iranian forces, particularly those who had penetrated in the direction of Hoveyzeh.

The Iranian attack clearly was ill-conceived and poorly executed. It may have been attempted because of pressure from the clerical establishment, which in the days preceding the attack had demanded that Iran launch a "final" offensive. The clerics may have been concerned about the impending hostage release and were looking for a quick diversion for public opinion.

Phase three of the war, which began approximately in early May 1981, has been characterized by a series of local Iranian offensives and victories, the most significant of which have been in the southern sector. Most of these initiatives have occurred in the area along the Bostan-Susangerd axis, although the Iranians have also been active around Abadan. During this period, the Iranians have achieved four significant victories. The first was at Susangerd in May. (See point 1, map 4.) As indicated previously, Iraqi forces had enveloped Susangerd on three sides, with the northern flank of the Iraqi forces dug in on the ridges of the Allah Akbar hills. Control of these hills is the key to the control of Susangerd and the surrounding region.

Iranian forces made a frontal assault on the Iraqi forces defending the Allah Akbar hills. At the same time, other Iranian forces attacked the Iraqi troops that were located directly west and southwest of the town. The fighting lasted approximately three days. When it was over, the Iranians had driven the Iraqis from the Allah Akbar heights and pushed the Iraqi forces several kilometers further west of the city. Susangerd itself was now securely in Iranian hands.

For the Iranians, the Susangerd offensive was significant for two reasons. Tactically, it laid the ground work for the Iranian thrust toward Bostan, which occurred later in the year. Without control of Susangerd, this later Iranian offensive would have been impossible. Psychologically, the second Susangerd campaign was a morale booster because it was the first Iranian victory of any major significance.[23]

A second major Iranian counteroffensive occurred at Abadan. (Point 2.) On September 29th, the Iranians attacked the Iraqi forces still positioned south of the Karun river. The battle was over by the 30th and ended with the disorderly retreat of the Iraqis back across the Karun. The siege of Abadan was now virtually lifted, with regular road communica-

Map 4

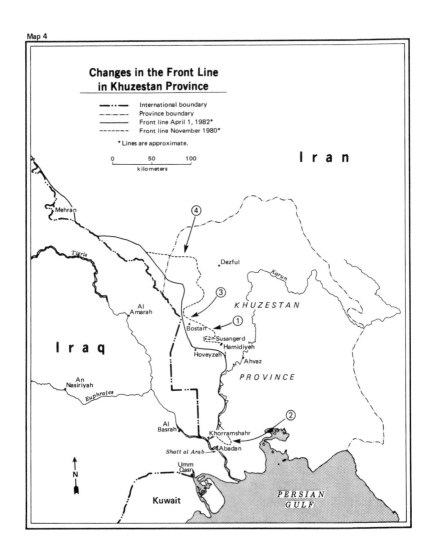

Changes in the Front Line
in Khuzestan Province

—··—   International boundary
—·—·—   Province boundary
————   Front line April 1, 1982*
- - - - -   Front line November 1980*

* Lines are approximate.

0   50   100
kilometers

I r a n

Mehran

Tigris

Dezful

Karun

④

Al
Amarah

③

KHUZESTAN

I r a q

Bostan

①

Susangerd
Hamidiyeh

Hoveyzeh

Ahvaz

An
Nasiriyah

Euphrates

PROVINCE

Al
Basrah

Khorramshahr

②

Shatt al Arab

Abadan

Umm
Qasr

N

Kuwait

PERSIAN
GULF

tions restored with Bandar Khomeini. The Iraqis, however, still remained entrenched in Khorramshahr and around the northern approaches to that city.

The Abadan victory added to the growing Iranian confidence. Speeches in the Majlis by various Iranian leaders predicted the collapse of Saddam Husayn and argued that such victories demonstrated that God was truly on the Iranian side. The victory may have also spurred the Iranians to strike at a Kuwaiti oil facility on October 1. The Iranians may have reasoned that the Gulf states would be less willing to support Iraq now that Iraq was "on the run" and Iran had again demonstrated its displeasure with Gulf state behavior. (If this were Iranian reasoning, it nevertheless failed to produce the desired results.)

A third Iranian offensive occurred two months after Abadan in the Bostan area. (Point 3.) The battle itself lasted approximately a week, from November 29 to December 5th. Following the second Susangerd offensive, Iraqi forces had retreated and redeployed in the vicinity of Bostan, which is located just a few miles from the border. As in the two previous offensives, the Iranians gradually concentrated their forces and then launched a direct assault on the Iraqi lines. The Bostan fighting was intense, with heavy casualties and equipment losses on both sides. When it was over, however, the Iranians had reoccupied Bostan and seized control of the environs.

Bostan was a significant victory for the Iranians and has serious implications for Iraq. Communications and logistical links between Iraqi forces concentrated at Dezful and Ahvaz had been effectively cut. Rapid shifts of men and material between these two fronts are more difficult if not impossible to achieve. Moreover, Iranian encirclement of one of the bulges in the Iraqi lines was now an option. Second, the Iranians now fully commanded the road that ran between al-Amarah and the front. Supplies had moved along that road from al-Amarah to the Ahvaz force concentration. That route was now closed. Moreover the Iraqis were no longer free to outflank the Iranians further south and move supplies to Ahvaz across the open desert. Large tracts of swampland lie below al-Amarah on the Iraqi side of the border, thus, the Ahvaz forces must be resupplied from the far south.

A fourth Iranian offensive was launched at the end of March 1982 in the area west of Dezful. (Point 4.) This offensive was by far Iran's most ambitious war effort and was aimed at nothing less than destroying Iraq's entire northern front, which was now isolated from the rest of the Iraqi front following the victory at Bostan.

The Iranian offensive, which lasted approximately a week, was conducted in three phases. In hindsight, the first two phases appear to have been softening up exercises with the final thrust reserved for a devastating knockout blow, which forced the remnants of the Iraqi forces to withdraw almost to the border. The Iranians committed as many as 100 thousand troops to the battle, while Iraqi forces numbered approximately 70 thousand. Some 20 thousand Iraqis were taken prisoner, including several hundred officers.

The Iranian victory has several important military and political implications. Militarily, the Iranians are in a much better position to seize and hold a chunk of Iraqi territory if they so choose. The Iraqi town of al-Amarah, for example, is a potential target, although at this writing it seems unlikely that Iran has the desire to push that deeply into Iraqi territory. The Iranians are also in a much stronger position to attack the remaining Iraqi forces in southern Khuzistan. Finally, the victory has given the Iranian military a tremendous psychological boost, while almost surely increasing morale problems within the Iraqi forces.

Politically, the victory will strengthen the grip of the Khomeini regime, demonstrating once again that God is "truly" on Iran's side. The Iranians will also be less inclined to negotiate and will continue to press the war to achieve their ultimate goal of overthrowing Saddam Husayn. Meanwhile, Saddam Husayn's political prestige will be further tarnished and his political career cast further in doubt.

3

The War and Domestic Policies

Clausewitz has pointed out that war is (or should be) a political act conducted within a political framework for political ends. By its very nature, however, the conduct of war is a risky undertaking. Governments are less able to influence the course of events than in other "political" situations, in large part because the number of uncontrollable variables quickly multiplies.

History is replete with examples of war being successfully employed as an instrument for achieving political ends (Bismark's three wars of German unification for example). It is also full of examples of battlefield reverses proving to be the ultimate undoing of a regime or political personality (for example, Czarist Russia or, more recently, Lyndon Johnson).

When the Iran-Iraq war commenced, conventional wisdom assumed that, in the case of Iran, battlefield reverses and the domestic political process would interact and automatically mean the quick demise of the Khomeini regime. As the war dragged on, and it became clear that Iran would not collapse, speculation shifted to the question of Saddam Husayn's long-term survivability. If Husayn were not able to win on the battlefield, how would that play politically in Baghdad? At this writing, (spring 1982), it is evident that thus far both regimes have been able to insulate the war—to a remarkable degree—from domestic politics and vice versa.[24] Interestingly, this situation has been particularly true of Iran; for example, the extraordinary political events that occurred in Tehran in the summer and early fall of 1981 were not a function of the war. On the contrary, Tehran politics had a momentum and life of their own and were governed by calculations and considerations having virtually nothing to do with the war.

Several factors have helped insulate the war from domestic politics. First, the same ideology that sustains the war continues to drive domestic politics. There is unity of purpose. Again, Iran provides the clearest example of this thesis. The war has fitted neatly into the overall ideological framework of the revolution. It is seen as an extension of Iran's grand crusade against "imperialism" because Iranians assume that the United States is the guiding force behind the Iraqi attack. More specifically, the war fits into the Shi'ite component of the revolution's ideology: According to Iranian broadcasts, against overwhelming odds, "good" (Iran) is struggling against "evil" (Iraq). Although an underdog in the struggle, good will ultimately triumph. Of course, there is a domestic counterpart to this siege mentality. Internal enemies who threaten the revolution must and will be overcome.[25] In Iran the same ideological underpinnings can serve the regime's military efforts and its domestic political policies.

In the case of Iraq, the underpinnings are not as explicitly linked; nevertheless, certain common ideological strands do exist. The purpose of the Iraqi Ba'thist regime is to serve the cause of the Arab nation. The war is part of that effort because Arab lands and rights are to be restored. This unity of ideology has contributed to the general insulation of the war from politics. Thus far, the conduct or purposes of the war are not issues that have split leading political figures. Again, Iran provides the best example of the phenomenon. Iranian political leaders have been clearly divided over the purposes and goals of the revolution, but not over the war. The extraordinary series of bombings, assassinations, and executions that occurred during the summer of 1981 were not precipitated as a result of a struggle over war policy. In fact throughout this period the Iranian war effort continued unabated.

The manner in which the war is being conducted at the front has also contributed to the separation between the war and domestic politics. First, after an initial phase of high-level military activity, the war has settled down to one of low-level intensity, although punctured by outbursts of intense activity. As a result, the expenditure of men and material has been reduced to the point where both sides seem willing to sustain current loss rates. Second, the air war gradually subsided so that civilian populations and economic (particularly oil) installations are no longer exposed to the rigors of the war. Third, there has been little effort by either side to cut off the other's economic and military resupply routes.[26] Thus, both countries have been able to maintain access to world markets, although during the hostage crisis Iranian access was, of course, severely restricted.

In reality, neither country has pursued an all-out war effort. Links between the front and the interior are thus reduced because neither country is fully mobilized. A crude "guns and butter" policy prevails, which has minimized civilian discomfiture and possible political fallout while allowing both sides to continue to strive "for total victory."[27]

The preceding analysis should not be construed to imply that there have been virtually no links between the front and the interior or that the war has not been used profitably for political purposes by both regimes. Rather, the argument is, in general, that the course of domestic politics and of the war has been sufficiently insulated thus far to allow the separate development of each without one gravely affecting the conduct of the other. Thus, political chaos could occur in Tehran and the front could hold. By the same token, although Iraq has not been able to win its expected quick victory, political repercussions have not developed as a result of this failure.

Both countries (but particularly Iran) have employed the war to serve political purposes. Initially, the Iranian regime used it to whip up enthusiasm for the revolution and the regime.[28]

Second, the war has provided an excuse for explaining away Iran's continuing economic paralysis. (Never mind that the Iranian government and the war have contributed significantly to this problem.) Officials ranging from Behzad Nabavi, minister of state for executive affairs, to bureaucrats within the various economic and development ministries have insisted that because the country is fully committed to the "war with imperialism," economic shortages and relocations will naturally occur. Moreover, the government cannot be held responsible for the stagnant economic situation as long as the war continues. Among the large segment of uneducated Iranians, such logic probably strikes a responsive chord.

The war has also kept the military pinned down on the country's geographic and political periphery and, therefore, out of politics. According to fundamentalist thinking, this situation is as it should be, because the fundamentalists have mistrusted the military from the early days of the revolution. Moreover, it is probably this desire to keep the military "preoccupied" that in part contributes to Tehran's willingness to prolong the war.

The existence of the war, however, has planted several seeds that over time might have important repercussions on Iran's political scene. At the ideological-propaganda level, the clerics have lost their claim to being the sole guardians of the revolution. They had argued that because they made the revolution, only they could preserve it. The war suggests otherwise. Such a shift in perception is subtle; its impact will not be immediately felt. But it is a deep running current that, when combined with several other factors, could chip away at the fundamentalists' armor.

On a more concrete level, the war has made a mockery of clerical calls for a phaseout of the military and of leftist demands for a purely people's army. Because of the war, the military will continue to function. Thus, it could possibly become a factor on the domestic political scene. Although the war may have helped revive the military, it has also strengthened its rival organization, the Revolutionary Guards. In addition to gaining battle experience, the Guards has also strengthened its command and control structure, learned to operate heavy weapons more efficiently, gradually developed an independent access to weapons and war materials, and strengthened its esprit de corps. Thus the Guards remains a formidable defender of the revolution and the current regime.

Finally, the war has severely undercut the efforts of exile groups to overthrow the regime. Former Prime Minister Shahpur Bakhtiar's public declaration that he was willing to help the Iraqi war effort if that was what was required to bring down the Khomeini regime was viewed on the home front as nothing short of a betrayal of Iran. General Gholom Oveissi also suffers from the same stigma of being too closely attached to or influenced by Baghdad.

A different situation exists in Iraq. The political situation is not fluid and power remains centralized. Saddam Husayn has not had to use the war to keep the military at bay, or as an excuse for any domestic shortcomings. There have been some political spin-offs, however, that have emerged in the wake of the war. The opposition Shi'ite ad-Da'wah party has from time to time stepped up its dissident activities. This was particularly true in the early days of the war, especially in southern Iraq. Kurdish dissidence has also re-emerged in the months following the outbreak of the hot war.[29] In both cases, however, these activities have not proven to be a threat to the regime, nor have they impinged on the Iraqi front-line activities in any manner.

There is one important sense in which concern about the domestic political situation has tempered Iraqi military activity. As indicated in chapter 2, for Husayn to win a strategic victory, he would have to be willing to pay a heavy price in men and material. The political price might be too high, however, because victory cannot be guaranteed, and large-scale losses without such a victory could simply not be justified. Moreover, Husayn has a particular problem in that much of the rank and file of the Iraqi army is composed of Shi'ite conscripts, a circumstance that has probably added to Husayn's caution.

Under what circumstances might a more explicit link be established between the front lines and the rear? In the case of Iran, the issue is reduced to the question of under what circumstances would the professional military become more directly involved in the political process. For the military to act, the level of chaos in Tehran would probably have to be substantially higher, the regime would have to be disintegrating visibly, Khomeini would probably have to be out of the picture, and the integrity of the military would have to be seriously threatened.[30]

An Iraqi offensive that would succeed in completely destroying the Iranian military is unlikely. It seems, therefore, that in Iran, the insulation of domestic politics from the war will change only if there are startling new political developments in Tehran.

For Iraq, the opposite situation appears to be true: the separation will be lessened more by events on the front than in Baghdad. Saddam Husayn's inability to win the war is a potential threat to him and to his regime. The real threat to Husayn probably comes from the Iraqi military and the Ba'th party. Frustration over the conduct of the war—perhaps precipitated by a string of Iranian tactical successes—might be the catalyst setting such a political process in motion.

4

Regional Responses to the War

Regional responses to the Iran-Iraq war have been varied—which is not surprising given the complex character of current Middle Eastern politics. In most cases, the response to the outbreak of hostilities was not determined solely on the basis of a government's direct reaction to the war or specific issues raised by it, but instead was strongly influenced by existing regional political dynamics, internal politics, and extraregional considerations, including superpower reactions to the war.

In turn, the war has influenced and molded the regional political environment, often accelerating the pace of various ongoing political processes. One example was the collapse of the coalition of Arab states opposed to Camp David. The coalition's unity had been disintegrating for several months prior to the war's beginning, but was given the coup de grace by the war.

The war has also demonstrated how difficult it is for the countries of the region to reconcile various ecumenical ideals and ideologies such as Arabism and Islam with basic national interests. Not all the Arab states for example have rallied to support their Iraqi brethren. Nor has Pakistan, which claims to be establishing a truly Islamic society, responded with unqualified support for Islamic Iran. In fact, in most cases hard core national interests have prevailed over more universalist impulses.

At the time the war broke out, several dissonant issues were of concern in the region. One issue was the fear of subversion. Arab states have often accused one another of meddling in each other's internal affairs. Mutual suspicion about externally sponsored internal subversion was particularly rampant in the months preceding the war. The Syrians were especially concerned about alleged Jordanian and Iraqi meddling.

A second issue was the unity of those Arab states opposed to Camp David. From November 1977 (at the time of Sadat's trip to Jerusalem) until December 1979 (the Soviet invasion of Afghanistan), the Arabs were united against Egypt. In turn, intra-Arab politics were relatively cordial and stable. (The Syrian-Iraqi fallout in the summer of 1979 was an exception—and a harbinger of the future.) This consensus broke down over the issue of whether to support the Soviets in international forums and elsewhere after their Afghan invasion.[31]

Uncertainty about superpower intentions in the region was another divisive issue, one of particular interest to the Gulf states. When the Iran-Iraq war began in earnest, both the United States and the Soviet Union were embroiled in confrontations in Iran and Afghanistan respectively. Would the war act as a catalyst for U.S. intervention or further Soviet adventurism?

Specific Responses

In general, the Arabian Peninsula States—those states geographically closest to the fighting and hence the most likely to become involved in it and excluding the Yemens—have been the vaguest in their *official* pronouncements toward the war, although this has not prevented them from extending material aid to Baghdad. Those states farther away—Syria and Jordan—have been much more explicit in their attitudes and much blunter in their official positions and actions.

The most immediate problem confronting the Peninsula states, once full-scale hostilities began, was whether to assume a quasi-neutralist position or openly support Iraq—support for Iran being out of the question. The decision had several implications. Certainly the Peninsula states wanted to see the Khomeini regime weakened, if not toppled. But a quick Iraqi victory would leave Baghdad the dominant political and military power in the Gulf. Failure to have enthusiastically supported the Iraqi effort from the start could incur the wrath of a now more powerful Baghdad. On the other hand, if Iran did not collapse, Iran might retaliate against the Gulf states. The decision about how to respond was made even more difficult once it became obvious that the Iranian air force was operational and prepared to strike at oil targets.

The Gulf states could not lightly dismiss the possibility of Iranian retaliation. Even before the war escalated to full-scale hostilities, a September 20, 1980 unattributed Iranian radio commentary fretted about the Peninsula states' failure to understand the true character of the border conflict:

> The dangerous route taken by certain Arab regimes in supporting Iraq's allegations against Iran is not justified by either evidence or argument. . . .The regimes that have supported . . . Baghdad both openly and covertly should have studied the situation well before proclaiming any support. . . .[32]

At this juncture, Tehran was complaining about the Peninsula states' moral support of Baghdad. On September 22 and 23, Iran expanded its warning. In a series of communiqués, the Peninsula governments (specifically "the UAE and some shaykhdoms") were warned not to aid Iraq by making available their harbor or airport facilities. Moreover, "Iran reserved the right to respond if they did so."[33]

The problem of how to respond to the war was complicated by two other factors: Saddam Husayn was insisting that the war was an Arab war that must have all-Arab support. Such a position could strike a responsive cord in the population at large. On the other hand, the Shi'ite population in states such as Bahrain or in Saudi Arabia's Eastern province could react negatively to a decision to give Iraq open-ended support.

Not unexpectedly, the Gulf states hedged their bets. They took action to support Iraq. Iraqi air force planes were given safe haven at airfields throughout the region. In addition, William Quandt has said that three states, Saudi Arabia, the UAE, and Oman, may have flirted with the idea of helping to support an Iraqi-organized seizure of the three Iranian-occupied islands in the Gulf.[34]

At the same time, the popular press in the Gulf was permitted to express what were decidedly pro-Iraqi opinions.[35] This action had the effect of giving Iraq "unofficial" support, thus helping to deflect Iraqi pressure for unambiguous official statements clearly supporting Iraq. It also allowed area governments to demonstrate to their local populations that they were not abandoning the Arab cause, while giving the leaders an opportunity to test and observe public reaction to the war. There were no official pronouncements explicitly and unreservedly supporting the Iraqi war effort. In fact efforts were made to stifle rumors that this was the policy. When a newspaper story broke that King Khalid of Saudi Arabia had called Saddam Husayn and assured the Iraqis of full Saudi support, Radio Riyadh attempted to set the record straight.[36]

As it became clearer that the war was settling down into a drawnout affair, statements from foreign ministries and high government officials in the Peninsula states tended to stress two general points: First, they were concerned that two Muslim nations were at war with each other. Second they urged both parties to find a quick, peaceful solution to the conflict. (A third and fourth point were often made as well: namely that the war diverted attention away from the struggle against Israel, and the war might permit the super-powers to intervene in the region.)[37]

These statements were certainly not endorsements of either of the combatants' war efforts and goals, rather they were an attempt to avoid deeper involvement in the war by not becoming publicly committed to Iraq. An official endorsement of Iraq could force the Iranians to make good on their retaliation threats. Moreover, this official distancing probably reflected a deep-seated concern about Iraq's ultimate political intentions and about the nature of Iraq's future relationship with the Peninsula.

Obviously, the attitude of Saudi Arabia was crucial in determining the posturing and policies of most of the Peninsula states toward the war. In general, the smaller Peninsula states would follow the broad outlines of the Saudi lead. Although Saudi policy was difficult to determine with precision, apparently within several days of the war's commencement Riyadh decided that it would remain officially neutral. (The ambiguous nature of King Khalid's phone call to Saddam Husayn was indicative of this position.) Specifically, Riyadh would not openly support or sanction Iraq's war aims and goals. At the same time, however, the Saudis quietly provided Iraq with various types and amounts of material aid.

Several factors probably influenced this decision, including concern for the oil fields, fear that the war might spread, and, at the worst, result in superpower intervention

or confrontation, and unease about long-term Iraqi intentions. Saudi neutrality, though, would be spelled with a
small "n," rather than a capital "N." Although the Saudis
may have harbored some long-term concerns about Baghdad, they were not prepared to remain so neutral as to deny
total support for an Arab brother. Moreover, the Saudis
probably wanted to keep Baghdad on its moderate, anti-
Soviet course, a path from which Iraq might stray were it
left completely alone.

The Saudi policy thus had a somewhat ambivalent qual-
ity to it: Riyadh would be neutral, yet aid Iraq. To fashion
such a policy was one matter, however; to implement it and
assure its success was quite another. In fact, the Saudis did
not have the necessary resources available to them to make
the policy workable. Saudi air defenses, for example, were
not capable of effectively detecting or neutralizing the Iranian air force should Tehran decide to attack Saudi oil fields.

It is within this context that the decision was probably
taken to invite the United States to send four Airborne
Warning and Control System (AWACS) planes. The
AWACS provided the underpinning for the Saudi neutrality; they allowed the Saudis to put some teeth into their
policy. Iran would be deterred from attacking the Saudi oil
fields, not only because Iranian aircraft could be tracked before they even left their airfields, but also because the mere
presence of U.S. planes in Saudi airspace increased the risk
of attack for Iran. Thus, the war could be contained.

At the same time, the AWACS decision permitted the
Saudis to pursue a policy of selective support for Iraq. Statements of official support for the war would not be made. Iraq
would not be in a position to pressure the Saudis to make
them because of Saudi Arabia's new independence derived
from the AWACS. Yet the Saudis would provide the Iraqis
with crucial material support in several areas. Iraq would
have access to world markets through a Saudi land bridge

running from the Red Sea to Iraq; financial aid would be forthcoming, (the Saudis and other Arab states have already given Iraq several billion dollars) and oil production would be increased, in part to help supply Iraqi customers who had been cut off by the war. The Saudis may have also requested the AWACS for a much more subtle reason as well. The AWACS presence has permitted the United States to protect Saudi oil indirectly. This passive role (one that has probably helped contain the war) has thus forestalled the need for a more active U.S. presence in the area, including possible large-scale U.S. intervention.

The desire to prevent a highly visible U.S. (or Soviet) presence in the region constitutes a basic tenet of Saudi foreign policy. It is also an attitude shared by most other regional states. The war threatened that policy because it was the first really critical event in contemporary Gulf history that, potentially, could cause serious physical damage to the Gulf oil fields and thus threaten Western oil supplies. How the United States would respond and was unclear. Certainly, the United States had announced it was prepared to intervene to protect those supplies. Although the Carter Doctrine of January 1980 was directed primarily at the Soviets, it was, nevertheless, vague, and "corollaries" to the doctrine were always possible.

If the Peninsula states wanted to blunt the temptation to intervene because of the circumstances created by the war, they would have to be able to assure the West that the oil fields were protected. Oil field security was best assured by containing the war and detering Tehran. The AWACS provided the best solution to that problem, although such a decision admittedly increased the U.S. presence.

In announcing the decision to ask for the AWACS, the Saudis sought to demonstrate that the request was not a radical departure from previous Saudi defense and foreign policy thinking, that it had a historical basis to it and was not done solely in response to the war. Prince Sultan ibn'Abd al-Aziz Al Saud, the Saudi defense minister, indicated for example, that "in the past, we approached Washington with a request to get such aircraft [in order] to raise the capability of the air forces of the Saudi Armed Forces."[38] Moreover, the AWACs had already visited Saudi Arabia previously; there was a precedent for their being on Saudi soil.

Syria and Jordan

The Syrian regime's decision to support Iran stemmed from both self-interest and self-preservation. Although it is true that the leadership in Damascus is drawn from the Alawite faction, which is Shi'ite in orientation, it would be a mistake to see the Syrian reaction as simply an extension of concern for their Iranian Shi'ite brothers.

Basically, the war threatened to isolate Syria in the Arab world, particularly if it were to result in an Iraqi victory. The developing Riyadh-Amman-Baghdad axis would have been strengthened; this, in turn, would seriously undermine Syria's claim to be the true leader of the Ba'th movement. Moreover, Syrian isolation could subject the regime of President Hafiz al-Assad to Israeli pressure, damage Syria's attempt to be the chief broker on the Arab-Israeli issue, and perhaps even ultimately loosen Damascus' control over the Palestinians, although this would not occur immediately. Furthermore, internal dissidents might be encouraged to redouble their efforts to overthrow the regime in the wake of these foreign policy setbacks.

All of these possibilities were not lost on the Syrians, and the public response to the war was correspondingly sharp. Iraq was roundly condemned for starting the war—a war that diverted Arab and Muslim attention from Israel—

the central issue of concern. Syria also acted as a conduit for weapons (primarily from the Eastern bloc) and for medical supplies going to Iran. The Jordanian reaction was unequivocal. Total support was given to the Iraqi war effort and its goals. But more than just political and moral support was offered; Jordanian port facilities at Aqaba were made available to Baghdad, and a land bridge was quickly created for embargoed Iraq. Iraqi aircraft were also flown to Jordanian air fields for safe haven. Finally, in early 1982, King Husayn announced that Jordanian "volunteers" would be urged to go to the front.

Several factors influenced Amman's decision to give open support to Iraq. The Jordanians hoped to continue to wean Baghdad away from its radical path. Also, an Iraqi victory might increase Jordanian maneuverability on the Arab-Israeli issue, perhaps even providing Jordan with a more assertive role.[39] If King Husayn ever aspired to such a role (and there is no available evidence to confirm or deny this possibility), he would have to neutralize or win support from Syria. An Iraqi victory would go a long way toward accomplishing that end. Finally, the war offered the chance of toppling Khomeini, something King Husayn had long desired.

It was against this background that the Jordanian-Syrian border crisis occurred in late November-early December, 1980. The Syrian perception of its isolation and vulnerability had probably increased following Damascus' ill-fated attempt to postpone a mid-November 1980 Arab summit meeting. (The summit agenda called for a discussion of the war, a discussion that Syria opposed). At any rate, the Syrians responded at the end of the month by massing troops along the Jordanian border. Jordan countered with its own military buildup, and the saber rattling continued for several days.

Ostensibly the Syrian buildup was intended to dissuade Jordanian backing of Syrian dissidents intent on overthrowing the Assad regime. Actually, the Syrian move was a political statement with a direct but simple message: Syria was still a principal power in Middle Eastern politics and its views could not be disregarded. More emphatically, Syria believed it should have the key role in the Arab-Israeli question.[40]

The Syrian move, therefore, was not designed to support the Iranian war effort, nor were the Iranians able to take advantage of the crisis. The result was that the war only intensified Syrian isolation and a drift toward a Jordanian-Iraqi-Saudi axis.

The Special Problem of Kuwait

When great powers argue, small powers always face the possibility of becoming involved in the dispute against their will. The more strategic value that a small power possesses, whether because of geographic location or resources, the greater the risk of becoming involved. Although the small Gulf shaykhdoms have generally been able to avoid being drawn deeply into the war, the war has nevertheless illuminated some of the potential vulnerabilities to which these small shaykhdoms might be subject. In particular, the war has shown that Kuwait's geostrategic importance has mixed blessings.

Traditionally, Kuwait's security policy has consisted of a series of balances; domestic policies have had to account for the large number of non-Kuwaitis resident in the country, many of whom are Palestinians. At the regional level, Kuwait has sought to remain on good terms with all the Arab leaders through generous aid donations. By doing so, Kuwait has sought to assure that all Arab states have a vested interest in its continued existence, thus hopefully forestalling Iraqi adventurism. Finally, Kuwait has sought to balance its superpower relationships by maintaining diplomatic relations with both Washington and Moscow. The balances are delicate and often subject to conditions beyond Kuwait's control. At the regional level, the traditional military balance between Iraq and Iran has provided the basis for Kuwait's policy of containing Iraq. The shah was committed to maintaining the status quo, and, as long as the balance remained, Iraq was not in a position seriously to pressure Kuwait. The balance of power between Iraq and Iran, however, was (and is) a relationship over which the Kuwaitis have virtually no control.

The war has buffeted Kuwait "between Iraq and a hard place." Even if it wanted to, Kuwait would have difficulty resisting Iraqi demands for access to port facilities and land transit rights. At the same time, Kuwait has not been able to defend itself against the limited Iranian military attacks. Moreover, to ask Iraq for defensive aid is not a solution, because such action could establish a precedent for the future—particularly should there be another conflict between Iraq and Iran. It might mean the first step toward the emergence of a de facto Iraqi protectorate over Kuwait.

The war has also made clear to Iraq some important geostrategic realities. At a minimum, it has raised again the contentious issue of control over the Kuwaiti islands of Bubiyan and Warbah, which dominate the entrance to the Iraqi port of Umm Qasr. In the summer of 1981, Saddam Husayn again reasserted Iraq's interest in gaining some type of control over these islands, an interest Iraq had expressed for at least five years. The war has demonstrated the importance of a coastline for Iraq. The Iranian navy has been able to bottle up Iraq easily, in part because of the limited Iraqi coastline. What this war may do is graphically demonstrate to Baghdad the geographic importance of Kuwait. Although an overt Iraqi seizure of Kuwait is unlikely, eventually Iraq may try to establish a special relationship with Kuwait.

The UAE and the Island Dispute

The advent of the war also witnessed renewed Iraqi efforts to become more involved in a dispute over islands between Iran and the UAE, although the latter has sought to prevent Iraq from becoming involved. The islands, Abu Musa and the Greater and Lesser Tunbs, are located at the western end of the Strait of Hormuz. Ras al-Khaymah and Sharjah claim the islands, which were occupied by the shah's troops in December 1971.

When the war broke out, Iraq suggested that one of its war aims was to liberate the three islands. The Iraqis may have seen the island dispute as a vehicle for becoming more involved in the UAE's foreign policy. Moreover, if Iraq could force the return of the islands, it would lend support to the idea that Iraq was the Peninsula's protector. Finally, if the island issue became intimately linked to Iraq's war goals, it would help "Arabize" the war.

The UAE soft-peddled the island issue, however. It failed to comment publicly on the self-proclaimed Iraqi goal and did not encourage Iraq to pursue its aim either militarily or in the negotiating process. In response, Iraq pressed the issue from time to time, apparently hoping to generate a positive response from the UAE. This public pressure continued throughout the autumn of 1980. Finally, in early December, the UAE declared that it intended to raise the island question in the United Nations and ask that body to examine the entire problem. In a message to UN Secretary General Kurt Waldheim, the UAE's UN representative indicated that the UAE wanted to maintain good relations with Iran, but insisted on restoring the UAE's sovereignty over the islands. The representative called upon Iran to change its attitude and prove its goodwill by respecting the sovereignty of the neighboring states. Finally, he expressed the UAE's willingness to negotiate "with the Iranian government to put an end to the problem."[41] By selecting the United Nations, the UAE could respond to Saddam Husayn's criticism that the UAE had failed to push the island issue and could avoid bringing Iraq directly into the dispute. The UAE message was clear as to which countries were parties to the dispute—the UAE and Iran. The UAE's initiative has not produced any results—the UAE never formally presented the matter—but the UAE may not have expected any. Its main concern seems to have been to prevent any further Iraqi involvement in the problem.

The Israelis and the War

Israeli security interests have been enhanced by the war, because the conflict greatly constricts Baghdad's ability to maneuver within the region. When Iraq made the decision to go to war with Iran, it opted out of the Arab-Israeli conflict as a significant participant. That Iraq can continue to oppose Israel on a propaganda level or confront Israel on diplomatic or economic levels is not at issue. Rather, Iraq's ability to directly threaten Israeli security on the military level has been significantly reduced.

Iraq's decision to go to war with Iran has meant—and will continue to mean—that Iraqi security is intimately tied to its eastern border and that it will not be capable of detailing any more than token military support to the Arab-Israeli front. (Israeli military planners will of course still have to be cognizant of Iraqi military capacity.) Thus, it will continue to be in Israel's interest to prolong the war or, once the fighting stops, to encourage a high state of tension between the two countries.

Israeli behavior during the war supports the preceding assertion. Israel has supplied Iran with arms and spare parts to assure that Iran can sustain its military effort. The war probably also encouraged the Israelis to strike at the Iraqi nuclear facility in June 1981. First, the Iraqi defences (particularly air defences) were trained on Iran. From that perspective, Iraq would never be more vulnerable defensively. Second, the Israelis probably calculated that Baghdad would be incapable of responding to the raid in any serious fashion. Saddam Husayn would not be in a position to threaten any drastic action because he was too tied up in his war with Iran.

Pakistan and the War

Pakistan's response to the war provides a clear example of the problem of trying to accomodate both Persian and Arab interests and aspirations. Islamabad has enormous financial and security interests in Iran and the Arab world. Pakistan's economic links with the Gulf Arab states are a vital component of the Pakistani economy. A vast number of Pakistanis work in the Gulf, sending home roughly $2 billion in foreign exchange. The oil-rich Arab states including Iraq have also given Pakistan direct financial aid. Finally, Pakistan is developing a military relationship with the Gulf states, particularly with Saudi Arabia.

The Pakistanis also have important security concerns in Iran. In the days of the shah, Pakistan used Iran as a balancer in Pakistan's relations with India. Iran, of course, is no longer able to function in that capacity; however, Iran and its revolution still have important security implications for the Pakistanis. Pakistan has a substantial Shi'ite population, which dictates that Islamabad develop at least a working relationship with the Khomeini regime. At the same time, Pakistan has wanted to insure that the two countries coordinate policy responses to the Soviet invasion of Afghanistan. In particular, Pakistan has wanted to maintain the same or essentially parallel responses to any Soviet-Afghan proposals for ending the crisis. The outbreak of the war posed a possible no-win situation for Islamabad. Support for one country would inflame the other. Like so many other parties, Pakistan attempted to be neutral. Almost immediately after war began Pakistan proclaimed that the war did not serve the interests of any of the Muslim states. Thereafter, General Mohammad Zia-ul-Haq (along with Secretary General of the Islamic Conference Habib Chatti) made the first mediation visit to the region, and Pakistan has continued to serve on the Islamic Conference's mediation team.

The Gulf Cooperation Council

The war also acted as a catalyst for the establishment of the Gulf Cooperation Council, although the Council certainly did not spring into existence simply because of the war. There had been talk about the need for some type of supra-Gulf body for several years. In the early 1970s, the shah had proposed a Gulf security pact. Various other schemes had been floated from time to time by Oman (1979) and Iraq (1980). None of these efforts ever came to fruition, however, primarily because the various states could not agree on the scope, nature, or even membership of such a regional body. The Peninsula states were suspicious that Iraq or Iran would dominate any organization of which they were members.

It was during the two to three years preceding the 1980 war that the Peninsula states gradually came to realize that some type of regional organization was needed. The Iranian revolution, the mosque incident in Mecca, and the Soviet invasion of Afghanistan encouraged such thinking, as did fear of superpower intervention. The perception developed that there was more that united the Gulf states than divided them. They all wanted internal security and stability to assure political survival and to maintain oil production. They were also concerned about increasing superpower tensions in the area, and some states may have hoped that the Council could provide an alternative to a U.S. military presence in the Gulf. Finally regional rivialries such as those being rekindled between Iraq and Iran were seen as a threat.

The outbreak of the Iran-Iraq war amplified those already existing concerns. At the same time, though, the war provided the Peninsula states with a unique opportunity. They could establish a regional body without inviting the two combatants to join because the two were at war. Under normal circumstances, it would have been impossible to establish a regional body without at least Iraq's participation. But now, under the guise that the Council was open to neutrals only, the issue was finessed past both countries. (Of course, the formula leaves open the possibility that Iraq and perhaps even Iran could join the Council in the future.)

In the late fall of 1980, there were several indications that the Peninsula states were considering establishing some type of cooperative body. On November 26, 1980, Dubai's *al-Bayan* quoted Saudi Interior Minister Nayif ibn 'Abd al-'Aziz Al Sa'ud as saying "There are plans for achieving Gulf security which, God willing, will become agreements soon. Saudi Arabia is trying to have a unified agreement on Gulf security." Nayif went on to indicate that Saudi Arabia did not rule out the possibility of convening a summit to discuss issues of interest.[42] Shortly after the Nayif statement, King Khalid told the Amir of Kuwait that the security of any regional state was indivisible from that of another and that "the security of Kuwait and Saudi Arabia are one."[43] On December 10, Saudi Defense Minister Prince Sultan commented that there was a need "for the existence of a joint defense strategy." Sultan noted, however, that such a strategy should be set within the context of the "Arab states as a whole," not only among the Gulf states.[44]

These latter statements may well have been made to mute Iraqi concerns about the possibility of the establishment of a cooperative council, the course and direction that it would take once it began to function, and the possibility that Iraq might be excluded from such a grouping. Iraq voiced its concern by invoking Arab unity. On November 30, 1980, Riyadh Radio quoted Iraqi Foreign Minister Sa'dun Hammadi as saying that Arab countries do not need an Arab defense pact to defend the Gulf because "those countries were bound together by the joint Arab defense treaty which secures their solidarity with each other in the event of any danger which threatens an Arab country."[45] Implicit in that statement is the concern that the Gulf states were preparing to establish some type of an exclusive security pact, which presumably would not include Iraq.

Despite Iraqi concerns, the Gulf states (Saudi Arabia, Oman, Kuwait, Bahrain, Qatar, and the UAE) pushed ahead with the Council project, and, in early February 1981, the Council was officially announced. Three ministerial conferences and various committee meetings were subsequently held during the year. The Council is not a formal security or military alliance such as NATO or the Warsaw Pact; initially, the members planned that it would coordinate and share information on political and economic issues. The Council has subsequently added defense-related issues to its agenda. Council members have also accelerated their efforts to coordinate internal security policies and have become increasingly concerned about Iran's intention to export its revolution.[46]

The Council has gone to great lengths to explain that it is not a defense pact and that it is not directed against any particular state. It has also pointed out that the Council does not violate the Arab League charter because there is a provision in the charter that says that member states can enter into other agreements among themselves.

The creation of the Council is probably one of the most significant political developments in the Peninsula of the past ten years. Its creation reflects a growing concern over the course of events as they have developed in the preceding years and the need for some type of arrangement to ward off both domestic and foreign threats. The Council's success is not assured. Internal bickering and differences persist. Moreover, when the Iran-Iraq war eventually comes to a close, the Council will have to face the issue of Iraq's admission. (It is unlikely that the Council would permit Iran to join or that the Iranians would have any interest in doing so.)

Arguments against Iraqi participation have centered primarily on the fear that Iraq would seek to dominate and control the Council. The longer the Council functions as an institution and the more of its basic institutions that are established, the less the entrance of Iraq is likely to be opposed on these grounds. Positive arguments for admitting Iraq flow from the belief that, if Iraq were a member, it would be less inclined to renew its pressure on Kuwait.

5

The War and the Superpowers

When the war began, Washington and Moscow found themselves in strangely parallel positions:

• In contrast to the Arab-Israeli wars, neither superpower was deeply committed to either combatant.

• Both powers had limited influence or ability to control the course of the war or bring the war to a close. It is true that the Soviets had access to the Iraqis, which the United States did not have, but that entré has had little impact on Iraq's behavior.

• Neither superpower has had any particular desire to see one side win decisively. A victorious Iraq would continue its evolution away from the Soviet Union. It would foster its leadership pretentions in the Gulf—a role that would not serve U.S. interests. A victorious Iran would continue its "neither East nor West" policy and prepare to engage in a more adventurous foreign policy.[47]

• In general, both superpowers recognize that Iran is the strategic prize in the region, not Iraq.

The result of this situation has been that both superpowers have responded to the war in similar ways.

The U.S. Response

Several factors conditioned the U.S. response to the Iran-Iraq war. The impact of the war on the hostage crisis was of immediate concern, for the war could not have come at a more awkward moment in that crisis. Early in September, the first major break in the hostage affair had occurred when U.S. Deputy Secretary of State Warren Christopher and other U.S. administration officials met in West Germany with Sadiq Tabatabai (who had connections to Khomeini) and discussed the broad outlines of a hostage settlement. In what appeared to be a positive Iranian response to that meeting, Khomeini publicly stated for the first time on September 12, 1980 the conditions under which he was willing to settle the crisis.[48] In these circumstances, Carter officials were concerned about keeping the dialogue on track to bring the crisis to a close as quickly as possible.

The Iranian decision to bomb Iraq's oil facilities and Tehran's threat to punish other states that aided and abetted Iraq quickly brought into sharp focus another U.S. policy concern: the need to contain the war to protect world access to Arabian Peninsula oil resources. Coinciding with this concern was an equally important consideration. The United States wanted to avoid a superpower confrontation while preventing the Soviets from taking advantage of the crisis to enhance Moscow's prestige and position in the region.

In hammering out a response to Khomeini, the U.S. government operated under several constraints. To keep the hostage dialogue alive, the administration had to demonstrate to Iran that, at a minimum, the United States was pursuing an evenhanded approach to the war. But an approach that was evenhanded or even remotely suggested a tilt toward Iran had risks. U. S. domestic public opinion was in no mood to see Iran handled gently, and such a perception could threaten President Carter's reelection campaign. Additionally, a perceived tilt to Iran had ramifications for U.S. policy in the Arab world. There has always been a deep-seated Arab perception that the United States is fundamentally anti-Arab. Until the Iranian revolution, Arabs believed the Washington-Tel Aviv-Tehran axis to be an anti-Arab alliance. If the United States were somehow to tilt even remotely toward Tehran in the Iran-Iraq war, the fundamental anti-Arab character of U.S. Middle East policy would be confirmed beyond all doubt.

The fact that the United States had virtually no influence in either Tehran or Baghdad was a second factor severely limiting U.S. ability to shape the direction and pace of events. Moreover, the United States had no serious capability for intervening militarily to produce a resolution of the conflict.

Despite these constraints, the elements of a U.S. policy toward the war rapidly emerged. On the day that the fighting between the two countries significantly escalated (September 21, 1980), Secretary of Defense Harold Brown set the stage by noting that the fighting had serious global implications and by implicitly suggesting that it did not serve the interest of any party.[49] By the 22nd, it was clear that full scale war had indeed erupted between the two countries. The Carter administration's official response to that development was to declare that the United States would be neutral toward the conflict and support its quick resolution. The president himself took the lead in articulating that stance by noting that "we are not taking a position in support of either Iran or Iraq. Our only hope is that the two nations can resolve the situation peacefully. We'll do everything we can do to contribute to that peaceful resolution."[50] Later that day, a State Department press spokesman commented that not only was the United States neutral but that the United States also saw no link between the war and the hostage issue.[51] By publicly decoupling the two issues,

Washington was signaling Tehran that it would not attempt to use the war to pressure or punish Iran because of the hostage issue and that the United States was prepared to continue the negotiations.[52]

The following day, September 23, the Carter administration's public pronouncements introduced two additional policy themes: containment of the war and avoidance of a superpower confrontation. These objectives reflected the heightened concern in Washington that if the war spread to the Arabian Peninsula, because of Iranian attacks on the Peninsula's oil facilities, the United States could not stand idly by. A direct clash between the United States and Iran raised the prospect (however remote) of a possible confrontation with the Soviets, a confrontation that would dash all hopes of a resolution of the hostage crisis. Thus the president strongly "encouraged all other countries, including the Soviet Union, not to interfere in the conflict." Having urged that the war be contained, Carter reemphasized that "the United States itself is following such a policy" (of neutrality.)[53]

Linked to the U.S. desire for containment of the war and avoidance of a superpower clash was the administration's desire to bring the fighting to a quick close. Thus, on September 24, Secretary of State Edmund Muskie stated that the pursuit of a "ceasefire resolution," which the U.N. Security Council was considering, was the "first priority" of the United States. Muskie acknowledged, however, that given the state of relations that existed between the United States and Iran and Iraq, Washington would be unable to take the lead in pushing a resolution through the Security Council.[54]

On September 24, the Carter administration also made explicit its concern that it was imperative that the West continue to have access to Arabian Peninsula oil resources. There were two basic ways Iran could threaten access to Peninsula oil. They could bomb the oil installations or close the Strait of Hormuz. The possibility of a strike was implicit in Tehran's warnings to the regional states on September 22 and 23. On the 23rd, Iran issued two communiqués that had serious implications for the Strait. In the first, "the heroic nation of Iran is informed that the Strait of Hormuz and the northern coasts of the Persian Gulf are under the control of the Armed Forces of the Islamic Republic of Iran." The second communiqué stated that, "bearing in mind the violations of the Iraqi Armed Forces, all waterways near Iranian shores [presumably including the Strait as well as the Shatt al Arab] are hereby declared war zones."[55]

There was an implicit policy in the two statements. Within the war zone controlled by Iranian forces, Iran could act in any manner to protect its national interests. Presumably closure of the Strait would be a policy option that Iran could exercise if its national interests so dictated.

The hint about restricted access to or a closure of the Strait implicit in the Iranian declaration elicited a quick response from President Carter: "Freedom of navigation in the Persian Gulf is of primary importance to the whole international community. It is imperative that there be no infringement of that freedom of passage of ships."[56] Carter implied that the Strait was so important to the global community that no state could close that body of water under any circumstances.

Thus, within the first three or four days of the war, the Carter administration had articulated publicly all of the constituent elements of its policy toward the war: neutrality, containment, cessation of hostilities, continued access to Arabian Peninsula oil, and avoidance of a superpower confrontation. In the days and weeks that followed, these skeletal elements were further developed. On September 25, the United States announced that it was holding up the planned shipment of several G.E. turbine engines that were to be used in Iraqi frigates being built in Italy.[57] Administration officials claimed that such a move was a logical outcome of U.S. neutrality. In this respect the move balanced the U.S. arms embargo to Iran, while trying to keep alive the hostage negotiations.

To reinforce the administration's view that the Strait must remain open, Carter declared on September 26 that the United States was willing to convene a conference of its major allies to discuss the Strait and a Western response to its closure.[58] It was soon clear that the United States was pushing ahead with the organization of a joint flotilla to protect the Strait.[59] But before the proposed flotilla became operational, the United States (and Western) posturing on the subject had its desired impact. On October 1, Tehran dramatically announced that the Strait would remain open, that it would be responsible for keeping the Strait open, and that Iran would resist any attempt by any power to close it.[60]

The meeting of Secretary of State Muskie and Soviet Foreign Minister Andrei Gromyko in New York in late September was also an occasion on which the United States reiterated its concern that all outside powers remain neutral toward the conflict and, in particular, refrain from resupplying either side with military arms and equipment. Finally, the decision to send the AWACS to Saudi Arabia flowed directly from the administration's concern about containing the war while maintaining access to the oil.

There were no departures from the Carter administration's basic policy during the remainder of its tenure in office. Nor has President Ronald Reagan's administration significantly shifted from the basic Carter orientation. President Reagan made it clear almost immediately that the United States intended to remain neutral toward the war and not supply any military related equipment to either combatant, including equipment that had been purchased by Iran and was awaiting shipment. In late October 1981,

Secretary of State Alexander Haig reiterated that the United States has "in the conduct of the Iran-Iraq conflict taken an impartial view . . ."[61] Moreover, the Reagan administration's willingness to hold exploratory talks with Baghdad in the spring of 1981 and its removal of Iraq from the list of countries supporting terrorism has not resulted thus far in any reversal of policy toward the war, despite Iranian propoganda to the contrary. The AWACs program, of course, has also been expanded.

The Soviets and the War

The Soviet response to the war was conditioned by Soviet global policies—more specifically by the role that the Middle East and particularly the Persian Gulf plays in furthering those policies. On a global level, the Soviet Union wants to preserve the security of the Soviet state and its empire while simultaneously creating a world environment that is conducive to Soviet political, economic, and ideological interests.

The geographic proximity of the region, particularly the Gulf, has obvious security implications for Moscow, albeit implications that the West can view both positively and negatively. A ring of states closely tied to the United States to the south of the Soviet Union could force Moscow to divert resources, particularly military resources, to its southern borders. On the other hand, weak, pliant states on the southern border mean that military resources can be channeled to other areas such as Western Europe and China. Moreover, a region of powerless states could serve as a platform from which Soviet power and influence could be directed toward Africa and South Asia.

Aside from geography, the oil reserves of the Persian Gulf have both an economic and political attraction for the Soviets. Barring a significant change in the structure and capability of the Soviet petroleum industry, at some point in the next 10 to 15 years the Soviet Union and Eastern Europe will probably become net importers of petroleum. The Persian Gulf would be a logical source of supply for the Soviets and Eastern Europe. This potential dependence heightens Soviet interest in developments in that region and their desire to influence those developments.

The Soviet interest in access to Persian Gulf oil is not reserved for some date in the future and for themselves alone, however. Their East European allies are currently almost entirely dependent on oil imports. While the Soviets now supply much of this oil, they have indicated that they would like to see their clients obtain more crude on the international market. Again, the Persian Gulf is the obvious source of supply, although it is not the only one.

It is not just the economic aspects of Persian Gulf oil that have attracted the attention of the Soviets. Western dependency on Persian Gulf oil provides Moscow with a potent political lever. Soviet control or influence over production levels, allocation flows, and prices could mean significant political power and could provide Moscow with an important wedge for separating Western Europe and Japan (both of whom are heavily dependent upon Gulf oil) from the U.S. security umbrella. Such an accomplishment would significantly enhance the prospects for achieving Soviet global interests and aspirations.

Soviet policy toward the region has been based on these various Soviet interests. The broad policy goal in the region is to hasten the decline of Western influence in the area while increasing Moscow's influence. Moscow can achieve this by encouraging the states in the region—through such means as coercive diplomacy, propaganda, and aid—to move from a pro-Western to a nonaligned stance (and perhaps eventually to an outright pro-Soviet stance). Once the Gulf states recognize the Soviet Union as a party with regional interests as significant as those of the United States, they will have to consult Moscow in all important regional issues. Soviet failure to achieve this goal raises the possibility of Soviet military intervention (particularly in Iran) with all of the attendant risks of a direct confrontation with the United States. Moscow has more specific policies for the various countries in the Gulf region. In Iran, the Soviets would probably like to achieve preponderant political influence. Such a position would reduce Soviet defense concerns, provide a platform for further pressure on the surrounding region, reestablish Soviet access to oil and gas supplies (probably on favorable economic terms), make port facilities available, and further enhance the Soviet claim to be a regional power.

At this juncture, Soviet policy aims in the Gulf may be more modest. On the Peninsula the Soviets probably want to improve access and influence through diplomatic representation. In Iraq, the Soviets want to preserve such influence and access as they have enjoyed in the past.

In responding to the war, the Soviets wanted to maximize their basic regional policy objectives. But they could probably not achieve such a goal without incurring political penalties. The fundamental problem was that the war raised the possibility that Moscow might have to choose sides at an inconvenient time. On the one hand, Moscow has supported the Iranian revolution as a means of ingratiating itself with the mullahs. Moscow's support did not extend to Iranian schemes for exporting the revolution. On the other hand, Moscow pursued a parallel Arab policy, which emphasized support for Arab causes and amicable bilateral relations.

The war was a complication. If Moscow gave its treaty ally, Iraq, full support, Iran would be enraged, and if Iran became desperate enough, the mullahs could turn toward the West. As it turned out, Iran accepted Israeli military aid. Failure to support Iraq, however, would only worsen the already cooling Soviet-Iraqi relationship. In the year or so preceding the outbreak of the war, the views and interests of Moscow and Baghdad had diverged in several areas, including trade and economic matters, political affairs (particularly over Afghanistan and regional security), and arms purchases.[62] A decisive tilt toward Iran offered potential strategic gains, particularly if Iran disintegrated under the impact of the war. Moscow would be much better positioned to pick up the pieces. Such a course of action had associated costs, however. In addition to losing Iraq, a significant tilt would alarm the Gulf states, which view Iran as a threat, and would significantly reduce if not eliminate Moscow's hopes of increasing its acceptability in the Peninsula. An Iranian tilt would reinforce the U.S. claim that the Afghan invasion was indeed another step in a series of offensive moves into the region.

Therefore, in framing a policy toward the war the Soviets took the line of least resistance. They acted as though they were neutral, although they made no official statement specifically outlining such a position. Instead, propaganda emanating from Moscow stressed that only "the imperialists" could gain from such a mutually destructive war. Soviet President Leonid Brezhnev commented that "neither Iraq nor Iran will gain anything from mutual destruction, bloodshed and the undermining of each other's economy."[63] On September 23, the Soviet newspaper, *Izvestia*, claimed that the United States was seeking to exploit the war to gain control of the region's oil while weakening Iran's ability to resist U.S. pressure on the hostage issue.[64]

Soviet neutrality was in fact somewhat of a tilt toward Iran, because the Soviets did have a treaty of friendship with Iraq. By not supporting their ally, the Soviets were in effect saying they disapproved of Iraq's action. The depth of that disapproval appeared in concrete Soviet behavior in the following days and weeks. First, Iraq's number two political figure, Tariq Aziz, received a cool reception when he visited Moscow immediately following the outbreak of the war. Then, in early October, the Soviets turned back two Iraq-bound Soviet arms ships that had actually entered the Persian Gulf.[65] Finally, at the end of October, the Soviets proceeded to conclude a treaty of friendship with Syria, Baghdad's traditional political foe. In the resulting joint Syrian-Soviet communiqué, Baghdad's actions were implicitly criticized. Of course, the treaty with Syria was, itself, a sign of displeasure with Iraq.

In general, the Soviets have maintained this posture throughout the war. They have from time to time attempted to strengthen their relations with Iraq. For example, when the large Iraqi electical power plant at Nasiriyyah was bombed in the early spring of 1981, the Soviets (who had built the plant) helped Iraq repair the damage quickly. Moreover, the Soviets seem to have permitted the resupply of some minor pieces of military equipment. Nonetheless, the general policy of neutrality has remained in effect.

To say that the Soviets have been essentially neutral in the war does not imply that they have not tried to use the conflict as a means of furthering their political interests and ambitions in the Gulf area. On the contrary, they have used the backdrop of the war as an occasion to reintroduce two schemes dear to the heart of the Kremlin: an all-European conference on energy and a plan for demilitarizing the Indian Ocean and Persian Gulf.

Brezhnev had floated the all-European energy conference idea in early 1980. Soviet commentator Nikolai Portugalov then elaborated on Brezhnev's remark in a TASS article on February 29, 1980. Noting that the United States, Western Europe, Japan, and—quoting West German Chancellor Helmut Schmidt—the Soviet Union all have legitimate rights of access to Persian Gulf oil, Portugalov proposed an all-European conference on energy under the auspices of the Conference on Security and Cooperation in Europe (CSCE) to guarantee secure and equal access to the oil. Under this plan, the CSCE members would submit proposals to the United Nations and to the Middle East oil-producing countries for approval. Portugalov contrasted this "constructive" resolution of the problem with "the adventurist and hegemonistic policy of the United States in the Persian Gulf region."

In a different slant, TASS First Deputy Director Sergei Losev in a March 5, 1980 broadcast called for an international conference on the Indian Ocean as a way to guarantee the security of the supply lines for Middle East and Persian Gulf oil. He suggested a somewhat different forum from the one Portugalov proposed, but the appeal for negotiations was the same.

The rationale for negotiations—but no specific proposal for them—was repeated by senior political pundit Aleksandr Bovin in *Izvestiya* on April 12. He argued that the USSR did not need Middle Eastern oil, but understood the West's need for it. He, too, underscored Moscow's assertion that the United States was responsible for insecurity in the area.

In mid-April, the Soviets began to develop a second scheme—the convening of a conference composed of countries of the Indian Ocean and Persian Gulf to discuss regional security issues. This proposal actually appeared as part of the Afghan Central Committee's program of April 17, 1980. Moscow, however, almost certainly approved and inspired the Afghan statement. In any case, the idea was incorporated into the Afghan Peace Plan of May 14, which has since become the basic negotiating position of the Soviets on Afghanistan.

Neither idea was favorably received in the West or in the Indian Ocean region, and the Soviets let them drop. With the outbreak of the war in September 1980, however, the Soviets reviewed both concepts. In October, at the Warsaw Pact foreign ministers' meeting, the oil conference idea was revived with the comment that the war lent additional urgency to the problem of oil security. On an early December visit to India, Brezhnev articulated a series of principles that, in the Soviet view, should govern the superpower approach to Persian Gulf security. All powers would agree

• Not to set up military bases in the Persian Gulf and on contiguous islands and not to deploy nuclear or any other weapons of mass destruction there;

• Not to use or threaten to use force against the Persian Gulf countries and not to interfere in their internal affairs;

• To respect the status of nonalignment chosen by the Persian Gulf states and not to draw them into military groupings of which nuclear powers are members;

• To respect the inalienable right of the region's states to their natural resources;

• Not to create any impediments or threats to normal trade exchange and the use of maritime communications connecting the states of this region with other countries.[66]

The Brezhnev speech did not specifically call for a formal security conference, although the thrust of the speech would suggest that the Soviets would welcome such a move.

When examined closely, the Brezhnev proposal appears to be a variation of a long standing Soviet plan for an Asian collective security pact. When stripped of its rhetoric, the collective security plan would establish that the Soviet Union is an Asian power with Asian security concerns, force the Western countries out of the region because they are not

Asian, and establish a basis for collective military *intervention.*[67] The idea was first given form in March 1972, when Brezhnev asserted that

> the real road to security in Asia is not the road of military blocs and groupings, not the road of opposing some states against others, but the road of good neighborly cooperation by all interested states. Collective security in Asia, as we see it, should be based on such principles as renunciation of the use of force in relations among states, respect for sovereignty and inviolability of borders, non-interference in internal affairs, extensive development of economic and other cooperation on the basis of full equality and mutual advantage.[68]

Many of the same themes found in the 1972 speech can also be found in the 1980 Persian Gulf proposal: noninterference in internal affairs, respect for sovereignty (both economic and political), and avoidance of limited military alliances or blocs. This idea is implicit in Brezhnev's call for no military bases in the area and explicitly in his call to "respect the status of non-alignment chosen by the Persian Gulf States." Although Brezhnev called for the Persian Gulf states not to be drawn "into military groupings of which nuclear powers are members," presumably this would not preclude the Gulf states' participation someday in the larger collective security scheme. By definition a collective security organization is not a military pact directed against a specific state or group of states.

Two factors probably influenced Moscow's decision to revive its oil conference and regional security schemes. First, by October 1980, the Western naval buildup in the Indian Ocean was moving ahead. The implication was that the West, alone, would be responsible for oil lane security in the crucial Persian Gulf region and that the Soviets would not be asked to participate as an equal partner with equal interests. Second, by late November various Gulf state leaders had made several public references to the necessity for establishing some type of regional organization. Given the Western orientation of these states, the Soviets probably feared that an essentially anti-Soviet pact, was about to be established, hence the necessity to develop the Brezhnev alternative.

6

Negotiation Efforts

Almost as soon as the war started, third party mediators undertook to arrange, at a minimum, a ceasefire or, on a more ambitious scale, to facilitate negotiations that would lead to a comprehensive settlement. All of these efforts foundered, primarily because neither side felt compelled to make enough concessions to produce a negotiated agreement. In the first year or so of the war both combatants' negotiating behavior indicated that they believed that their war aims could best be obtained on the battlefield. Viewed from a slightly different angle, there were no meaningful concessions from either side because the cost of pursuing the military option was not so high that concessions seemed an attractive way out. Furthermore, the political risk that either regime ran if it obtained less than "total victory" was considered more threatening than continuing the war.[69] Under these circumstances, serious negotiations could occur only when one side achieved a strategic victory and was in a position to enforce a settlement or when both sides decided that a continuation of the war was more costly than a settlement.[70]

If neither side is capable of delivering the critical

knockout blow, it seems clear that when serious negotiations do commence there will be at least four distinct issues that will have to be confronted. The first issue is military in nature and is related to finding a mutually acceptable ceasefire and withdrawal sequence. The Iranians have held that a ceasefire must be followed by an immediate withdrawal of all Iraqi forces from Iranian territory. Negotiations on outstanding differences can then follow. Behind this demand lies Tehran's belief that it is the "innocent," and hence morally righteous, party. Iran should not have to negotiate the removal of foreign troops from its soil. Lurking behind this "holier than thou attitude," however, may be the fear that the pattern of Arab-Israeli ceasefires may be repeated: a ceasefire occurs but does not lead to the evacuation of the enemy's forces.

Not unexpectedly, Iraq has argued for a sequence that calls for a ceasefire, then negotiations, then a withdrawal. Negotiations would focus on such probems as the Shatt al Arab river and noninterference in the internal affairs of each state.

The remaining three issues are political in nature. The first concerns the Shatt. Basically, the Shatt issue is composed of two facets, with the sovereignty issue dominating. Baghdad wants full sovereignty over the Shatt and thus, at a minimum, has insisted that the border be drawn on the basis of the 1937 treaty. Iran continues to demand that joint sovereignty must be exercised over the river; therefore, the thalweg principle as specified in the 1975 treaty must continue to apply. A second facet of the issue concerns the uses of the Shatt. How are the Shatt's waters to be governed? Although the 1937 and 1975 treaties called for commissions to work out arrangements covering this general topic, substantive efforts were not made to implement those provisions of the two treaties.

A second major problem to be resolved is the development of a common position on the issue of noninterference in the internal affairs of each country. Iraq launched its invasion, in part, because it saw an Iranian hand in such events as the attempted assassination of Vice President Tariq Aziz in the summer of 1980 and in antigovernment demonstrations that occurred in the Shi'ite quarters of various Iraqi cities in the months following the collapse of the shah. Iranian propaganda broadcasts calling for the overthrow of the Ba'this only reinforced this perception. By the same token, Iran has charged that Iraq was aiding and abetting ethnic minority dissidence and was responsible for several oil pipeline explosions. Thus both have demanded a cessation of intrigue while proclaiming their own innocence.

A final issue to be resolved is Iran's insistence that a commission be formed to investigate the question of who was responsible for the war and to determine war reparations.

The Mediators and Their Plans

Several efforts have been initiated to arrange either a ceasefire or full-fledged settlement. A week after the Iraqi invasion, the UN Security Council passed Resolution 479 calling for an immediate, in-place ceasefire. Iraq, having occupied a substantial chunk of Iranian real estate, not unexpectedly agreed to abide by the resolution, provided Iran did so. Iran, on the other hand, denounced the resolution. The Iranians thought the United Nations should have condemned Baghdad as an aggressor and called for an immediate Iraqi withdrawal.

Parallel to the UN effort, Yasir Arafat conducted a brief shuttle diplomacy, urging both sides to resolve their differences through negotiations. Arafat was genuinely appalled by the war because it threatened to divert attention from the Arab-Israeli conflict, split the Arab world, and put pressure on the Palestine Liberation Organization (PLO) to choose sides. For his efforts, Arafat succeeded only in offending both parties. Iran demanded PLO support in the name of Islamic unity, while Iraq demanded it in the name of Arab unity. In such a charged atmosphere, Arafat quickly withdrew.[71] Finally, the Islamic Conference swung into action on an ad hoc basis. Because most Islamic Conference foreign ministers were in New York attending the opening session of the UN General Assembly when the war commenced, an informal consulting group was established in New York. On that basis, President Zia-ul-Haq of Pakistan and Habib Chatti, secretary general of the Conference, were authorized to act as mediators on behalf of the Conference.[72] Chatti and Zia traveled to Baghdad and Tehran but were unable to modify the minimal negotiating demands of either party.

As the war became more stabilized, mediation efforts also took on a more formalized and structured character and were officially sponsored either by the United Nations, the Islamic Conference, or the Nonaligned Movement (NAM).[73] Although working separately, each group began to probe more systematically for openings that might lead to a comprehensive settlement package. UN Secretary General Waldheim then appointed former Swedish Prime Minister Olof Palme as his special representative, while the Islamic Conference assembled a fully functioning mediation team only after the Ta'if conference in January 1981. Similarly, NAM appointed a special committee following its foreign ministers' conference in New Delhi.

Several obstacles of a generalized nature have hampered the mediation efforts of these groups. For example, as the UN representative, Palme had to overcome Iran's deeply-held suspicion that the United Nations was pro-Iraqi and pro-U.S. in outlook. Moreover, each group also had to avoid becoming a pawn in Iran's ongoing power struggles.

Both the Islamic Conference and NAM had constraints put on them with regard to their selection of mediation team members. Iraq refused to meet with any mediation team that included any Arab members. Iraq was fighting for an Arab cause, not just for Iraq, and, under such circumstances, an Arab could not mediate when the Arab cause was at issue.

Baghdad's arguments seem to have been designed to prevent Algeria from being included on one of the teams. At the time, Algeria had just successfully shepherded the American hostage negotiations to a conclusion and had access to the various power centers in Tehran. Although such an entré could be a plus, Baghdad was concerned about Algeria's neutrality, fearing that the Algerians were pro-Iranian. The PLO eventually joined the NAM committee, however, with no apparent opposition from Baghdad.

On a deeper level, the fundamental problem that each mediation team faced was that neither side was interested in peace except on its own terms, although the Iraqi attitude may have changed. Thus, any plan that exacted significant compromises from both parties was deemed unacceptable. By the same token, a plan that tilted too much in favor of one party ran the risk of permanently alienating the other combatant. Although the necessary will to negotiate a settlement has been lacking, both parties nevertheless have been willing to receive the mediation teams. Public relations have entered into this decision, because each has wanted to avoid being labeled intransigent.

The bulk of the mediation activity occurred in the spring of 1981. Mediation teams were shuttling back and forth between Tehran and Baghdad, sometimes almost bumping into each other. Part of this flowering of activity was motivated by the fear that Saddam Husayn's much heralded spring offensive would shut off any chance of achieving success.

Mediation activity soon subsided, in part because the spring offensive failed to materialize. Other factors, however, also contributed to a dampening of efforts, including the death in late May of Bangledesh President Ziaur Rahman who was on the Islamic Conference team, the Israeli strike on Iraq's nuclear facilities, and the deteriorating political situation in Iran. As of March 1982, mediation efforts generally remain suspended.

Thus far, the Islamic Conference has produced the only comprehensive peace plan, in contrast to, say, the NAM team, whose basic approach has been to "listen" and try to determine common points of view. The first Conference plan contained two major sections.[74] Part one consisted of a set of principles that, taken together, would establish a general framework for governing relations between the two countries. These principles included respect for the sovereignty and territorial integrity of each country, the nonaquisition of territory by force, noninterference in the internal affairs of each state, settlement of differences by peaceful means, and freedom of navigation. In other words, these were basic principles by which the international community claims to be governed and thus should be readily acceptable to both parties with no loss of face.

Part two of the plan attempted to grapple with the thorny issues of a ceasefire, withdrawal, and negotiations on the Shatt al Arab. Initially, the plan proposed the establishment of two commissions composed of various Islamic Conference member countries. One commission (or subcommittee) would be responsible for implementing, maintaining, and policing a ceasefire and withdrawal, which would take place over a period of four weeks. (Islamic military observers would be employed throughout the process.) A second commission would establish a temporary regime for the Shatt and would supervise navigation on the river pending a final settlement.

Iran rejected the initial plan. In a March 6 interview, Ali Khamenei, then the Ayatollah Khomeini's representative on the Supreme Defense Council and president of the country, stated that there were three reasons for the rejection: First, the proposal did not contain any "specific basis and principle for settling the dispute. As far as we were concerned, the basis for a settlement of the dispute is the 1975 Algiers accord. Consequently, there is no point in negotiating the issue of the Shatt al-Arab again." Second, there was no mechanism available for investigating "Iraq's aggression." Third, "any agreement must emphasize that the aggressive forces must withdraw unconditionally. We cannot accept the idea of allocating a certain period between a ceasefire and the withdrawal of forces."[75]

In part because of the Iranian objections, the plan was modified. One commission would be responsible for implementing, maintaining, and policing a ceasefire. A second commission was assigned two functions: it was to determine the circumstances, the method, and the schedule for a withdrawal, while simultaneously drawing up a framework and agenda for negotiations on the Shatt dispute. Finally, a third commission was added to investigate the causes of the war.

The plan was ingenious and was a classic example of how a cover for disengagement could have been provided for both parties—provided the will to negotiate existed. First, the plan treated certain problems or potential problems as basic principles, which have been accepted by all nations and therefore were not subject to negotiations. For example, territory would not be acquired by force, thus, Khuzistan would be returned to Iran. Acceptance of the principle of noninterference in the internal affairs of each state would prevent recriminations. Further, adherence to the principle of freedom of navigation assured that both parties would have access to the Shatt, regardless of where a boundary line would ultimately be drawn. In its final form, the plan also attempted to finesse the issues of a ceasefire and withdrawal and the sovereignty of the Shatt. Iran had demanded that a ceasefire be followed by an immediate withdrawal, while Iraq has insisted that no withdrawal could occur until after Iran recognized Iraq's sovereign rights. The plan in fact decoupled the two component parts of each demand. The commission responsible for ceasefire arrangements would not be linked in any manner to the commission implementing the withdrawal procedures. The temporal link would be cut, although this did not imply that Iraq's troops would remain for an indefinite period inside Iran.

Concurrently, the plan did not endorse the Iraqi demand that its sovereignty over the Shatt be recognized before any withdrawal. On the contrary, the fact that one of the commission's explicit mandates was to draw up an agenda and framework for Shatt negotiations makes clear the Conference's position that all issues concerning the Shatt are negotiable.

The plan failed to gain full acceptance in both capitals precisely because it did decouple the basic demand of each side. Acceptance of the plan would have required concessions and would have been tantamount to acknowledging that neither party was a winner, even though neither side could have been tagged a loser.

Interestingly, Iraq did accept the idea of a commission to determine the aggressor. Although the commission was an obvious sop to Iran, Baghdad may have calculated that in fact Iraq had a credible case against Iran—or that it could tie up such a commission in paper and red ink for years to come.

UN Special Representative Palme generated the only

other concrete peace proposal. However, unlike the Islamic Conference proposal, his was much more limited in scope, concerning itself solely with the issue of freeing the commercial shipping that was trapped in the Shatt following the outbreak of hostilities. (Some 50 vessels were immobilized in and around the ports of Basra, Abadan, and Khorramshahr.) Early in his shuttle diplomacy, Palme apparently concluded that a comprehensive settlement could not be negotiated. He seems to have reasoned that if agreement could be reached on the issue of freeing the ships, it might establish an atmosphere of trust, which could eventually pave the way for a more comprehensive agreement.

In broad outline, Palme's plan would have divided the Shatt into sections that would be dredged and cleared one by one, apparently starting at the river's mouth. A ceasefire mainly aimed at preventing long range artillery duels would be declared in each sector where work was in progress. It is not clear how the ships would be freed, whether section by section or all at one time.

On the surface, it would seem that neither party could object to the release of third-country commercial shipping. Depending on the manner in which the release was to be implemented, however, certain aspects of the release could buttress each countries claim on the Shatt sovereignty issues. First, there was the problem of whose flag was to be flown when the ships left the Shatt. (When a ship passes through a country's territorial waters, the host's flag is flown.) Naturally, Iraq insisted that its flag be flown, reflecting its claim to full sovereignty over the river, while Iran insisted that both flags be displayed, reflecting its position of shared sovereignty. The problem was finally resolved when both parties agreed to let the ships fly the Red Cross flag.

A second complex question was who would pay for the dredging and clearing expenses. Again, reflecting their respective positions on the sovereignty issue, Iraq insisted that it alone would bear all the costs, while Iran demanded that the costs be split. Palme tried to maneuver around this issue by suggesting that a third party (for example, the ship owners) pick up the cost. At the same time, he tried to assure both parties that such action in no way prejudiced their respective claims. Unfortunately, the entire scheme foundered on the payments dispute, and the ships remained stranded.

7

The Implications of the War

The Iran-Iraq conflict will continue to be a major source of tension and instability in the Persian Gulf region for the indefinite future. Until the war began, the Gulf was an area of potential intraregional conflict. Now it joins the eastern Mediterranean (with its Arab-Israeli and Greek-Turkish conflicts) and South Asia (with the Indian-Pakistani conflict) as yet another region with an almost intractable dispute. While holding both countries in a hostage-like grip in the coming years, the conflict has the potential to erupt repeatedly into full scale hostilities and expand to neighboring states, particularly in the Arabian Peninsula.

The tension will persist regardless of how this phase of the conflict ends. Victory for one side will leave the other seeking revenge. Because it is extremely doubtful that the victor would have the capacity to occupy the defeated country or destroy its economic and military infrastructure, over the longer term the loser will eventually have the opportunity to attempt to reverse the outcome of this period of conflict.

An agreement negotiated because of mutual exhaustion could restore relations between the two countries to something close to the status quo ante; but it would leave both powers dissatisfied and probably ultimately unwilling to maintain a permanent peace. The underlying political issues of the war would not have been resolved, including the struggle for regional preeminence and the desire to alter the political status quo in each country. Thus, a negotiated settlement (regardless of the reasons that lead both parties to agree to it) would be more like an armed truce than a prelude to peace.

The persistence of this tension has several important implications, which, for analytical purposes, have military and political subsets. These subsets, however, are not strictly compartmentalized, but are often interconnected and overlapping. The major challenge of this continuing tension for U.S. policy is whether the United States can prevent further outbreaks of hostilities and whether it can help insulate the rest of the region from them if they occur.

Military Implications

The persistence of bilateral tensions will compel both Iran and Iraq to rearm or seek to rearm. That an arms race could ensue is obvious. In turn, the types of weapons or weapons systems that the two countries seek to acquire and the nature and structure of a supplier-recipient relationship could have an important impact on the course of a future conflict, the political relationships of each country with the Peninsula states, and the influence of the superpowers in the area.

Naval expansionism and rearmament might be a possible outcome. The superiority of the Iranian navy in the Gulf helped doom the seige of Abadan and shut down all of Iraq's crude oil exports through the Gulf. Its navy has helped protect Iranian crude exports, which are absolutely essential for Iran's shaky financial condition. Iran's naval superiority has demonstrated that it will be difficult for Iraq to play the leading role in the Gulf.[76] Thus an Iraqi drive for expanded naval capabilities and an Iranian determination to maintain its naval edge point to a possible area of arms competition. The expansion of both navies has political and economic implications, in addition to a military impact. The political power projection of both countries would be enhanced. If Iraq were able to acquire a "blue water" Gulf navy, its influence in the lower Gulf would be greatly expanded, with more direct competition with Iran in and around the Strait of Hormuz a likely spin-off. Greater pressure on Kuwait could develop if Baghdad insisted on a resolution of the issue of Bubiyan and Warbah islands; Iran could find itself in the somewhat ironic position of being sympathic to (if not outright supportive of) the Kuwaiti position.

If hostilities were to occur again, an expanded naval capacity on both sides suggest that the war would be carried into the Gulf itself. Such a development would very likely have a direct impact on oil production in the Peninsula. Under wartime conditions, the Gulf oil flow to the West could be interrupted by damage to the oil fields, high wartime insurance rates for tankers, producer-ordered shutdowns (because of perceived danger to the oil fields), and by blockades of the oil-loading ports or the Strait of Hormuz. If both sides acquire an enhanced naval capacity, all of these oil choke points could be affected.

The nationality of the armament supplier and the terms and conditions are also issues of critical importance. The Persian Gulf region is now one of the principal areas of superpower competition. This competition is heightened by the fact that Iran and Iraq are "grey areas," where superpower influence is amorphous and in flux. How each country responds to a possible arms race will affect the position of the superpowers in each country and will influence the overall prospects for regional stability.

Domestic Political Ramifications

The Arab-Israeli dispute is the fundamental issue that has defined the content, scope, direction, and pace of the political life of those states directly involved in that conflict. In much the same way, the tension between Iraq and Iran will tend to act as one of the central issues of political (and military) life in both countries. It will form a backdrop against which many (but not all) political issues will be defined for an indefinite period of time. Moreover, social and economic planning and their priorities will be influenced by the persistence of tension and the greater emphasis on defense spending. (There is a certain irony in all of this for the Khomeini regime because it had vehemently denounced the shah's military spending.)

Although an earlier chapter argued that thus far the war had not had a significant impact on domestic politics, a prolongation of the war could alter that situation, particularly in Iraq. By April 1982, Baghdad was on the defensive. The Iranians scored victories at Susangerd, Abadan, Bostan, and Dezful, despite Iraqi resistence and high Iranian casualties. If this pattern of Iranian victories were to continue, it could lead to a serious deterioration in Iraqi troop morale, desertions, and dissatisfaction within the officer corps and among the general population. As a result, Saddam Husayn's future could be at risk.

Who would succeed Husayn is an open question. The most likely possibility would be some coalition drawn from within the military or ruling Ba'th party. Other political forces exist, however: the Iraqi Communist Party has been suppressed, but not eliminated. It could yet raise its head. A second possibility is a Khomeini-style Shi'ite seizure of power. A Shi'ite organization, the ad-Da'wah Party, exists, despite government attempts to break it, but it has not represented a substantial threat, though that could change. An Iraqi Shi'ite victory would be particularly serious. Assuming that such a regime were to share the Iranian view that other governments in the region are illegitimate, it is likely that dissident activities in the Peninsula and elsewhere would be encouraged and supported.

There is the possibility that the war could have more pronounced political repercussions in Tehran if Iraq were again able to seize the initiative and inflict a series of significant defeats on the Iranians. Until that happens, however, it seems unlikely that the war by itself will produce political change in Iran. On the contrary, it has probably strengthened Khomeini's government.

Regional Political Implications

The persistence of Iranian-Iraqi tension will enhance and strengthen the role of Saudi Arabia in the political, military, and security affairs of the Gulf. The continuation of this conflict, however, is not the only factor influencing this development, because there is Peninsula-wide concern about Iran's oft stated goal of exporting its revolution.

The process of Saudi enhancement is already underway. Iraq has become increasingly dependent on Saudi Arabia for financial support. Riyadh, with Kuwaiti support, pushed through the establishment of the Gulf Cooperation Council and signed a series of bilateral security agreements with various Gulf shaykhdoms following the thwarting of an apparently Iranian-inspired attempt to assassinate much of Bahrain's royal family.[77] This increasing Saudi dominance suggests that the Gulf shaykhdoms will be more directly tied to Saudi foreign policy initiatives and positions than ever before. Saudi dominance also suggests that Riyadh may be in a strong enough position to prevent border disputes and other conflicts that exist among and between various states from developing into full-scale hostilities. The Saudis, however, have to be careful. If they employ their enhanced political influence in an arbitrary and heavy-handed manner, political tensions with the smaller Gulf states (particularly the UAE) could ensue.

Turning to the wider Arab world, the war has acted as a catalyst for yet another realignment of Arab politics. Ringing the region is the Steadfastness alliance, consisting of Syria, Libya, the PLO, and the People's Democratic Republic of Yemen (PDRY). Within the circle lies the Arabian Peninsula, Iraq, Jordan, and Egypt. Whether this configuration remains—or the circumstances under which it evolves—probably depends more on other broader issues, particularly the Arab-Israeli dispute, than on the state of tension existing between Iran and Iraq. Actions such as the Jordanian decision to send volunteer troops to the Iraqi front, however, will continue to exacerbate relations between the two blocks.

The gravitation of Iran toward the Steadfastness circle appears to be yet another spin-off of the war. Syria and Libya have offered military aid to Iran, which has been readily accepted. At the November 1981 Steadfastness summit, Iran was permitted to attend as an observer. Moreover, Iran and the PDRY have both expressed a desire to establish full diplomatic relations.

Although Iran has not entered into a treaty relationship with Steadfastness members, the closer links with these states nevertheless raises the possibility of closer coordination of foreign policies primarily for destabilization purposes in the Peninsula and Iraq and greater (but admittedly indirect) Soviet influence in Tehran. Iran has continued to refuse to engage in any discussion as long as Soviet troops are in Afghanistan. In time, Tehran's foreign policy could become more compatible with Soviet interests in the Middle East and Southwest Asia. Over the long term, Iran could mellow on the Afghan issue, perhaps even eventually engaging in talks on a political settlement prior to a Soviet withdrawal.

Toward a Regional U.S. Security Policy

In his State of the Union address on January 23, 1980, Jimmy Carter declared that the Persian Gulf region fell within the sphere of the United States' vital interests and that the United States would repel, "by any means necessary, including military force," an attempt by any outside force to gain control of the region.[78] The Carter Doctrine was formulated in response to the Soviet invasion of Afghanistan and was aimed primarily at deterring any further Soviet or Soviet-inspired expansionism.[79] Behind the U.S. concern about further Soviet expansionism into the area lay the U.S. fear about loss of access to Persian Gulf oil. This loss of access as a result of a direct Soviet seizure of the oil fields is only one facet of the access issue, however, and this is the problem with the Carter Doctrine as it now stands.

Access to oil can be threatened in at least four different ways. The first is a producer-inspired boycott such as occurred in 1973, during the October war, in which the flow of oil is curtailed or eliminated to achieve political or economic goals. The Iranian Revolution provides a second example of how access to oil can be endangered. As the revolution demonstrates, internal instability can severely restrict or halt the flow of oil. The Soviet invasion of Afghanistan is a third example of the access problem. Although the invasion did not actually impede the flow of oil from the Gulf, it has provided the Soviets with an improved staging post for yet another possible thrust toward the Gulf. Finally, the Iran-Iraq war has destroyed the myth that the producing states would never be so irrational as to destroy their economic lifeline. It also suggests that the oil production of noncombatants could be affected through war zone insurance rates or fears of retaliation.

Although the direct Soviet threat to the Gulf cannot and should not be ignored, the historical record shows that internal instability, such as in Iran, and regional tensions and instability, such as caused by the Iran-Iraq and the Arab-Israeli wars, have had the most direct and negative impact upon access to oil. Moreover, neither of these factors is destined to disappear in the 1980s; on the contrary, these types of issues may continue to have the most direct impact upon oil access in the coming years. A cessation of fighting in the Iran-Iraq war will not signal an end to the tensions between the two antagonists. A renewed outbreak of hostilities remains possible if not probable, raising once again the chances of the fighting spreading to the Peninsula states. The problem for U.S. policy is that the war has vividly demonstrated how limited U.S. leverage is. The United States was not able to control or defuse the border and other disputes that lead to the outbreak of the war, and it is not able to bring the combatants to the peace table. Nor is there any reason to believe that Washington's political leverage over Baghdad or Tehran will markedly increase in the future.

The experience of the Iran-Iraq war suggests that one aspect of a comprehensive U.S. security policy should focus on the issue of intraregional security. In its initial development, the policy might be predicated on the following assumptions:

• The Iran-Iraq conflict will continue to be the most important regional flashpoint, unless a fundamentalist Shi'ite regime emerges in Baghdad that might temporarily mend fences with Tehran.

• Iran and Iraq are or can be the most powerful countries in the region.

• They are also the two states most inclined to try to alter the political status quo in the region. This is particularly true of Iran at the moment.

• Conflicts between other states exist in the region such as border disputes and ethnic and tribal tensions. Of these conflicts, however, the most likely to occur in the future would probably involve either Iran (with Bahrain or with the UAE over the island issue) or Iraq (with Kuwait).

• The Peninsula states want to avoid entanglement in the Iran-Iraq dispute.

The basic aims of a U.S. policy in the region should be to moderate the future growth of uneven power and influence in both Iran or Iraq so that neither state would be tempted to try forcibly to attain regional hegemony and to help the Peninsula states resist becoming involved in Iranian-Iraqi disputes. The policy could be fashioned with northern and southern components. At the heart of a policy toward Iran and Iraq, the United States should seek a balance of power as a means of curtailing further adventurism, such as the temptation to renew hostilities following some type of settlement. The United States should remember that it was probably the perceived collapse of the balance of power that lead Iraq to contemplate war. The border conflict between the two states probably could have simmered indefinitely had Baghdad not thought that Iran was vulnerable and that the cost of attacking would be minimal. The purpose of the balance of power would be to prevent either country from achieving a preponderance of power on the northern littoral, while keeping both parties occupied with their disputed border.

At best, the United States has only limited capacity to achieve such a balance of power. To have any chance of success, cooperation with the allies would be necessary on a range of issues, including trade, economic development, and arms sales.

On the southern littoral, a regional U.S. policy could be developed around the concept of "splendid insulation." The basic thrust would be to encourage initiatives that would insulate the Peninsula states from the Iran-Iraq conflict. The strengthening of the AWACS role in the Peninsula contributes to their military security, hence, their "isolation." Another factor that would help would be the development of a redundant capacity in the oil fields—at pumping stations and loading facilities as well as with alternative pipeline routes. Various aspects of the redundancy issue, such as a pipeline that would bypass the Strait of Hormuz, are currently being discussed. Further discussion should be encouraged.

In evolving such a policy the Western allies should continue to make it clear that the Strait of Hormuz remains outside the compass of Persian Gulf power politics. As the "choke point" through which all Gulf oil must pass, the United States needs to discourage any party from using the Strait as a political weapon.

In reality, these ideas can probably only be imperfectly implemented. Yet they may provide some organizational concepts around which further specific policies toward Gulf regional security issues can be formulated. None of these ideas, however, would necessarily have any direct influence in promoting internal stability or preventing the export of the Iranian revolution. Those are issues for which separate policies must be created.

Notes

1. Wright, Claudia, "Implications of the Iraq-Iran War," *Foreign Affairs* (Winter, 1980-1981):277.

2. Broadly speaking, the thalweg principle states that the border of two states separated by a river should be drawn down the center of the major navigable channel of the river.

3. For example, both the shah and the Ba'this were, and are, secularists, who would modernize and develop their countries at the expense of so-called traditional values. The Iranian Revolution directly challenges that approach and defines the main issue of debate as one of Islam versus secularism.

4. Again, this observation does not pass judgment on whether the September 22 invasion was "defensive" and a response to earlier stepped-up shellings (as the Iraqis claim), or an "unprovoked" attack (as the Iranians suggest).

5. Wright, "Implications of the Iraq-Iran War," p. 279.

6. Foreign Broadcast Information Service (FBIS), Middle East and Africa (MEA), September 4, 1980, p. E:1.

7. FBIS (MEA), September 11, 1980, p. E:1-3.

8. FBIS, South Asia (SA), September 15, 1980, p. I:14.

9. "Since the rulers of Iran have violated this agreement as of the beginning of their reign by blatantly and deliberately intervening in Iraq's domestic affairs, by backing and financing as

did the Shah before them, the leaders of the mutiny which is backed by America and Zionism and by refusing to return the Iraqi territories which we were compelled to liberate by force, I announce ... that we consider the 6 March, 1975 agreement as abrogated from our side also." FBIS (MEA), September 18, 1980, p. E:5. Saddam Husayn's use of the phrase "from our side also" is curious, because it implies that Iraq was reacting to a similar Iranian declaration. Yet, Tehran had not officially abrogated the treaty, although Iranian leaders on occasion vaguely hinted that perhaps they were not bound to it. For example, on the same day of Husayn's speech, Agence France Presse published an interview with Abolhassan Bani-Sadr in which the Iranian president acknowledged that Iran had not implemented the 1975 treaty with regard to the territorial strips. But, he asked, "Who signed the treaty?" The implication was that the shah had signed it.

10. FBIS (MEA), September 18, 1980, p. E:5.

11. The full statement reads as follows: "What we demand is that the Iranian government openly, legally recognize the historical and legitimate right of Iraq over its land and waters. We demand that Iran adhere to good neighbor relations; abandon its trends of racism, aggression and expansion; abandon its evil attempts to interfere in the domestic affairs of the region's countries and return every inch it has usurped from the homeland ... We call on the Iranian Government to give up its occupation of the three Arab islands." FBIS (MEA), September 29, 1980, p. E:3.

12. FBIS (SA) September 29, 1980, p. I:6.

13. *Ibid.* September 23, 1980, p. I:3.

14. *Ibid.* September 23, 1980, p. I:7.

15. See Wright, "Implications of the Iraq-Iran War," pp. 278–285 for a discussion of Iraqi planning on the diplomatic dimension.

16. Wright, "Implications of the Iraq-Iran War," p. 286.

17. The loss of Abadan might have created a psychological loss, but not one sufficient to bring Khomeini down. Again, it should be pointed out that Abadan is an oil refining center; the oil fields themselves lie approximately 100 miles to the east.

18. Why did the Khuzistani Arabs support Iran? Although the question is extremely important, unfortunately there are no

readily confirmable answers, only speculative hunches. First, there is a large Iranian presence in Khuzistan. To revolt against Iran when its back was against the wall was obviously a dangerous proposition. The Iranian regime had demonstrated that it was willing to employ repression, particularly during the summer of 1979 when Admiral Habibulah Madani (now part of the exile movement) was governor of the province. The decision not to oppose Iran was probably reinforced when Iran did not collapse, which meant that there would be no quick Iraqi victory. Thus, the fence sitters were unwilling to risk their lives for what might be a losing cause.

There may, however, be a deeper-seated explanation for the behavior of the Khuzistani Arabs. It is possible that these Arabs (or majority of them) are in fact committed to the Iranian state and genuinely perceive themselves to be more Iranian than Arab. Whatever the reasons for their behavior, their reactions to the Iraqi invasion raise the general issue of whether or under what circumstances any of Iran's ethnic minorities can be successfully manipulated. On the basis of this one case, generalizations are difficult to make. The example of the Khuzistani Arabs bears close scrutiny, however.

19. Iranian war communiqués are full of references to the "Brother Guardsmen" who valiantly blew up an ammunition dump here or a gasoline truck there.

20. On September 22, the day the war began in earnest, the Revolutionary Command Council (RCC) stated that "We shall avoid striking at civilian targets unless the Iranian side persists in striking at civilian targets." (The RCC was referring to earlier Iranian bombing and shellings.) FBIS (MEA), September 23, 1980, p. E:9.

Despite the Iranian strikes on oil targets on September 23, the RCC still hinted that it was willing to avoid economic targeting. "We warn the racist . . . authorities in Iran that this is the final strong warning. If our civilian and economic targets are hit, Iraqi armed land and air forces . . . will deal deterrent strikes against Iranian economic installations in all areas." FBIS (MEA), September 24, 1980, p. E:7.

21. The following account of the war's military operation is necessarily abbreviated because of space requirements. Therefore

it only covers major events and trends. A more detailed military history of the war should someday be written.

The dates are admittedly somewhat arbitrary, and, in reality, one phase has gradually merged into the other. Moreover, there are overlaps in the phases. For example, there have been periods of stalemate such as during the summer of 1981 within phase three (the Iranian offensive). Despite these limitations, the phase notion is useful because it helps establish a mental construct for analyzing events and the broad trends of the war.

22. Bani-Sadr, for example, had made those charges on occasion in the months preceding the war.

23. Ironically, the victory could have been a factor that contributed to the military's willingness to side with Khomeini and the mullahs when the final assault was launched against Bani-Sadr.

24. That is not to say direct and explicit linkage is nonexistent. The disastrous Iranian offensive in January 1981 in the Susangerd area occurred around the time of the hostage release. Another offensive occurred in the same area shortly after the late August 1981 explosion, which sent President Rajai and Prime Minister Mohammad Bohanar to their deaths. In both cases, events in Tehran would seem to have produced a reaction at the front.

25. This perception of "good" struggling against "evil" is a classic Shi'ite motif stretching back to the very early stirrings of that movement.

26. Iran has bombed Kuwaiti territory on at least two separate occasions and seized, but later released, a Danish vessel bound for Kuwait suspected of carrying "contraband" material as a demonstration of its displeasure with Kuwaiti behavior. Specifically, the Iranians are incensed that Kuwait has been willing to act as an entrepôt for Iraqi cargoes. Beyond these isolated demonstrations, however, the Iranians have not interfered with Iraqi-bound traffic.

27. Iraq has probably been far more successful in the "butter" aspects of this policy. Reportedly, Baghdad is flooded with consumer goods and food—in fact, far more so than prior to the war. The construction industry is booming, and Baghdad is pressing on with its ambitious economic development programs.

Iran is not able to match this performance. Tehran, however, has been able to meet minimal needs. Iranians are not starving. An assortment of consumer goods are available, although on a much more modest scale. (Of course, part of this reduction of consumer goods availability is the result of deliberate government policy.)

28. In this respect, Khomeini and the revolution have been lucky. They came to power on an obvious revolutionary high. Some of this enthusiasm was gradually spent in subsequent months. The seizure of the American Embassy, however, fanned the fires of the revolutionary spirit. Just at a time when interest in the hostages was beginning to wane, however, the war came. A new symbol on which to vent revolutionary wrath had almost miraculously emerged.

29. In Iran, the Kurds have generally been unable to take advantage of the war. In fact, the situation in Iranian Kurdistan is about the same as it was prior to the war: The government controls key urban areas, the Kurds, the rural hinterland. Among themselves, the Kurds remain factionalized.

30. The experience of the war may have given the military the confidence (which was obviously lacking previously) to act.

31. For a fuller treatment of this topic, see Bruce Maddy-Weitzman, "The Fragmentation of Arab Politics: Inter-Arab Affairs Since the Afghanistan Invasion," *Orbis* 25, no. 2 (Summer 1981).

32. FBIS (SA), September 22, 1980, p. I:10-11.

33. The military communiqué on September 22 singled out the "UAE and some other Shaykhdoms in the Persian Gulf" (and not Saudi Arabia) as the Peninsula states that might allow Iraq to use their port (marine and air) facilities. A September 23 Ministry of Foreign Affairs' communiqué called on "the Islamic governments, particularly Iran's neighboring governments, not to allow their facilities and their air space, their waters or territories to be used by the infidel." Yet, another September 23 communiqué warned that Iran was not responsible "for ships and dockings with regard to any cargo belonging to the Baathist Iraqi Government transported through any port in the Persian Gulf." FBIS (SA), September 23, 1980, p. I:18, September 24, pp. I:5-6, 18.

Taken together, the communiqués were trying to establish

that Iran considered any support for Iraq (overflight privileges, sanctuaries for Iraqi military equipment, and entrepôt functions) to be a hostile act that invited retaliation of an indeterminate nature. The bombing of Iraqi oil facilities suggested a possible course of action, however.

34. William Quandt, "Reaction of the Arab Gulf States," in *The Iran-Iraq War: Issues of Conflict and Prospects for Settlement*, ed. Ali E. Hillal Dessouki, Policy Memorandum No. 40 (Princeton, N.J.: Center for International Studies, Princeton University, August 1981).

35. The Kuwaiti press was particularly anti-Iranian. Explaining that attitude was an article in the *Arab Times* of September 26, 1980, entitled "Khomeini Must Fall."

Not all papers were strident, however. In the UAE, *al-Ittihad* hoped that the Islamic states would be able to contain the war, while *al-Khalij* wondered if some third party were not benefiting from the conflict. Finally, the Dubai paper, *al-Bayan*, called on the Islamic Conference to promote an armistice. FBIS (MEA), September 25, 1980, pp. A:2-3.

36. Riyadh radio noted that Khalid had talked to Husayn but it stressed that Khalid had "expressed [to] President Husayn his interest and good fraternal feelings," and that views on the dimension of the current situation had been exchanged. Khalid was quoted as saying to Husayn that "I beseech God Almighty to guide our steps in the interest of our Arab and Islamic nation." FBIS (MEA), September 26, 1980, p. C-1.

37. On October 8, for example, Sa'd Abdallah Salim Al Sabah, Kuwait's crown prince and prime minister, called for a speedy ending of the battles between Iraq and Iran "and putting an end to the shedding of blood and the wastage of resources . . ." FBIS (MEA), October 9, 1980, p. C-1.

38. *Ibid.* October 6, 1980, p. C:2.

39. For example, during the fall of 1980, there had been unofficial speculation in the United States that the Jordanian card or option may be the next step in the peace process. Note the comments made by William Quandt at a conference hosted by the Middle East Research Institute of the University of Pennsylvania in November 1980.

40. Syria made the same point a year later at the November 1981 Arab Summit, which was to have discussed the Saudi peace proposals. The Summit was torpedoed after Assad refused to attend. Again, the central message was that Syria must be a partner in any Arab initiative involving the Arab-Israeli dispute.

41. FBIS (MEA), December 12, 1980, pp. C:2-3.

42. *Ibid.* December 5, 1980, p. C:1.

43. *Ibid.* December 1, 1980, p. V. At the time this statement was made, Kuwaiti officials denied that a Gulf pact was about to be signed.

44. *Ibid.* December 11, 1980. This same idea was echoed by Bahraini Prime Minister Shaykh Isa bin Salman Al Khalifa, who commented that it was necessary to find a system to safeguard the area, but "security of the region is an indivisible part of the total concept of Arab unity. Arab collective security is based on a national and not a regional outlook." FBIS (MEA), December 24, 1980, p. C:1.

45. *Ibid.* December 1, 1980. Summary of Events Section, p. V.

46. David Ottoway, "Allegation of Iranian Plots Increase Gulf Concerns for Security," *Washington Post,* January 2, 1982.

47. One could argue that the Soviets would have been willing to live with an Iraqi victory if they could have capitalized on the Iranian defeat by inserting a pro-Soviet regime in Tehran in the wake of an almost certain collapse of that regime. The United States might also have been able to do the same thing, however, a possibility that the Soviets could not discount.

48. Until September 12, 1980, Khomeini had never explicitly outlined his settlement demands, despite numerous tirades denouncing the United States and Jimmy Carter. Of course, other revolutionaries had ticked off a variety of settlement terms.

49. Brown commented that "it [the fighting] is very dangerous to both of those countries; is very dangerous to all countries in the region and is potentially dangerous to the peace of the world." *Washington Post,* September 22, 1980.

50. *Ibid.*

51. *Ibid.*

52. The Iranians, however, quickly linked the United States to the Iraqi attack. In a representative comment on September 21,

1980, Abadan Radio declared that "after Carter lost hope of dominating Muslim Iran and plundering its natural resources and plentiful minerals . . .he found his goal in activating the enemy of Islam, Saddam at-Takrite . . .In this way, he found a way to create trouble for the Islamic Republic [of Iran]," FBIS (SA), September 22, 1980, p.I:12.

53. *Ibid.* September 24, 1981, p. A-1.

54. *Ibid.* September 25, 1981.

55. *Ibid.* September 23, 1981, pp. I:13-14.

56. *Ibid.* September 24, 1981, p. A-1.

57. *Ibid.* September 26, 1981.

58. *Ibid.* September 27, 1981, p. 1.

59. *Ibid.* October 2, 1981. The allied flotilla eventually included ships from the United States, France, Great Britain, Australia, and Oman.

60. *Ibid.* October 2, 1981, p. 1. A foreshadowing of the Iranian position appeared a day earlier in an unattributed radio commentary. The commentary began by analyzing the importance of the Gulf and Strait for "world devouring imperialism [i.e., the United States] and by noting that the Gulf was absolutely crucial for the United States. The commentary then went on to say that "at this point, we are not going to deal with Mr. Carter's concern and the measures which these gentlemen are to take to protect the security of the Persian Gulf. (FBIS, October 1, 1980, pp. I:14-16). Although the language is oblique, the commentary was signaling that the Iranians recognized the importance of the Gulf to the United States and were not prepared to confront Washington.

61. "Remarks by the Honorable Alexander M. Haig, Jr., October 29, 1981." Released by the Bureau of Public Affairs, Department of State, October 30, 1981, no. 364, p. 15.

62. For fuller treatment of this topic, see Karen Dawisha, "Moscow and the Gulf War," *The World Today* 37, no. 1 (January 1981).

63. *Ibid.,* p. 11.

64. Quoted in Alvin Z. Rubinstein, "The USSR and Khomeini' Iran," *International Affairs* (London) 57, no. 4 (August 1981):610.

65. *Washington Post,* October 2, 1981.

66. A. Alexeyev and A. Fialkovsky, "For a Peaceful Indian Ocean," *International Affairs* (Moscow), (February 1981):87.

67. A. G. Noorani, "Soviet Ambitions in South Asia," *International Security 4.* (Winter 1979-1980):31-59. Most of the following discussion is based on the Noorani article.

68. "Soviet Review," March 28, 1971, quoted in *Ibid.*

69. Iraq's view on this general subject may be changing. In a December 15, 1981 speech before a meeting in Baghdad of labor ministers from the Nonaligned Movement, Saddam Husayn indicated that Iraq would agree to end the war when Iranian leaders were capable of recognizing Iraq's international borders as cited in international treaties approved by the two sides. (FBIS, Middle East/North African Report, December 16, 1981, p. E:1.) This statement suggests for the first time that the 1975 treaty could be a basis for conducting negotiations, although it might not be the only basis. Prior to this statement, Iraq had dismissed outright any possibilities of using the 1975 treaty in negotiations with Iran. Any use of the 1975 treaty, whether explicit or implicit, would hardly constitute a victory for Baghdad.

70. It will have to be a mutual recognition. If one side wants to continue the war and the other does not, the war party would have essentially the same negotiating leverage as if it had won a strategic victory.

71. A comment by Ayatollah Khomeini's son, Ahmad, revealed the scope of the problem for Arafat: "I told Brother Yasir Arafat: 'What I expect of you is that you clearly define your stance in regard to the issue of Iran-Iraq . . . In no way is it in your interest to talk about negotiations and other things and I am sure you will not.'" FBIS (SA), September 1980, p. I:18.

For the second time within a year, Arafat had alienated his new-found ally, Iran. (The first occasion was when Arafat attempted to intervene in the hostage crisis in its early days.) In both cases the Iranians thought that they were being asked to compromise or negotiate on issues that required no negotiation. In both cases, the Iranians believed they held the high ground, morally.

72. A day after the war began in earnest (September 23), Chatti indicated that, if called upon to mediate, his basic strategy would be to establish an immediate ceasefire (presumably in place)

and start negotiations to resolve differences. FBIS (MEA), September 23, 1980, p. A-1.

73. The Islamic Conference proposed to expand its two-man ad hoc team into a regular committee, according to an interview with Chatti on October 30. At the time, Chatti indicated that Iraq had accepted the idea but that the Iranians were hesitant. According to him, Iran objected because acceptance of a regular committee might be construed as violating the self-imposed principle of no negotiation before withdrawal. Iran did accept the Conference proposal subsequently. FBIS (MEA), October 31, 1980.

74. The text of the original is as follows:
A. The principles:
1. Iran and Iraq shall fully respect each other's national sovereignty and territorial integrity.
2. The Iraqi and Iranian sides shall restate that they do not accept the principle of the acquisition of territories by force.
3. Iran and Iraq shall reaffirm the principle of noninterference of either side in the internal affairs of the other in any form.
4. Iran and Iraq shall reaffirm their acceptance of the principle of settling international differences by peaceful means.
5. Iran and Iraq shall accept the principle of freedom of navigation in the Shatt al-Arab.
B. Elements of a comprehensive peace settlement:
1. The cease-fire between Iraq and Iran shall come into force on the night of Thursday, 13 March 1981 at 0000. [Sic]
2. The Iraqi forces shall withdraw from the Iranian territories on Fraiday, 20 March 1981, the withdrawal to be completed within 4 weeks in accordance with [the recommendations?] of a military subcommittee.
3. The cease-fire and the withdrawal of forces shall take place under the supervision of military observers acceptable to both sides from the member states of the Islamic Conference Organization.
4. The question of the Shatt al-Arab shall be submitted to a committee comprising members of the Islamic Confer-

ence Organization acceptable to both sides, Iran and Iraq, to detail the basic regulations for this waterway.

  5. Negotiations shall be held to find a peaceful solution to other differences following the withdrawal of the Iraqi forces from the Iranian territories.

  6. Decalarations shall be exchanged between Iraq and Iran on the noninterference of each party in the internal affairs of the other.

  7. The member states of the Islamic Conference Organization will undertake to guarantee each side's respect to its commitments based on a comprehensive peace settlement and the stationing of observers on both sides of the international borders of the two countries as and when necessary for a specific period.

  C. Temporary measures for ensuring freedom of navigation in the Shatt al-Arab:

  1. Commencing from the date when the cease-fire comes into effect and pending a final agreement, the Shatt al-Arab shall be under the control of a special body which is under the supervision of the Islamic Conference Organization.

  2. This special body shall be empowered to ask the Islamic Conference Organization to place at its disposal a peacekeeping force to assist it in its task of ensuring freedom of navigation in the Shatt al-Arab during this period.

  D. The Islamic good office committee shall set up a subcommittee to assist both sides to [carry out?] the measures for a comprehensive peace settlement. FBIS (MEA), March 5, 1981, pp. A:1–2.

  75. FBIS (SA), March 9, 1981, p. I:1.

  76. Andrew Pierre has observed that "history has taught us that states rarely achieve a significant political or economic rank without seeking commensurate military power." Andrew J. Pierre, The Global Politics of Arms Sales (Princeton, N.J.: Princeton University Press, 1981), p. 277.

  77. David Ottoway, "Allegations of Iranian Plots."

  78. The complete statement runs as follows: "Let our position be absolutely clear: An attempt by any outside force to gain control of the Persian Gulf region will be regarded as an assault on

the vital interests of the United States of America and will be repelled by any means necessary, including military force."

79. See David Newsom, *Foreign Policy* 42 (Summer 1981) for some interesting comments on the background of the Carter Doctrine. At the time, Newsom was under secretary of state for political affairs at the Department of State.

About the Author

Stephen R. Grummon is currently an International Affairs Fellow of the Council on Foreign Relations. He is on leave from the Department of State where he serves as an analyst on Iran for the Bureau of Intelligence and Research. He was a Peace Corps volunteer in Iran from 1970–1972. The author has an M.A. from the Johns Hopkins University School for Advanced International Studies, where he is also a candidate for a Ph.D.